Pacific Coast Highway

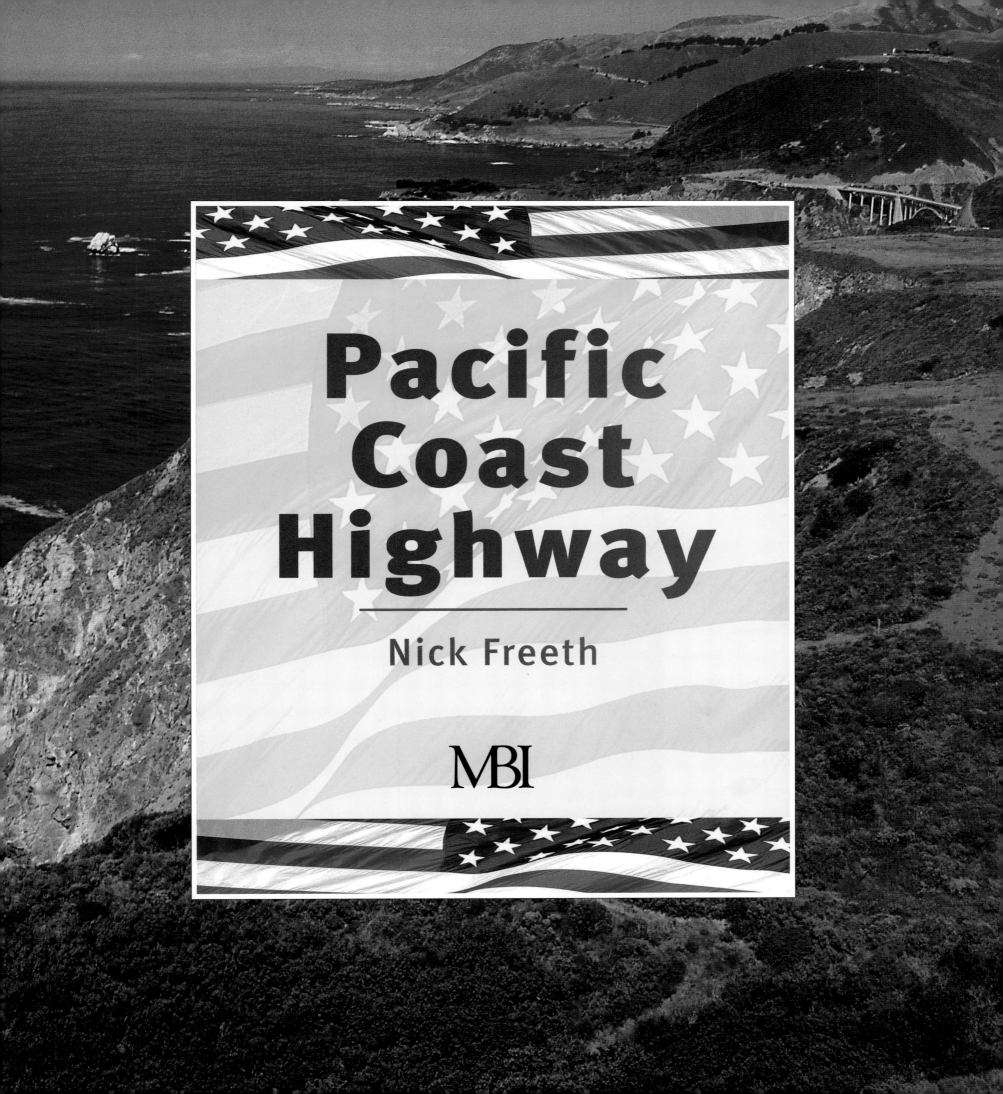

Pacific Coast Highway

Nick Freeth

MBI

EDITORS: **Katherine Edelston**
& Marie Clayton
DESIGNER: **Philip Clucas** MSIAD
PRODUCTION: **Ian Hughes**
PHOTOGRAPHER: **Neil Sutherland**
INDEX: **Dr Caroline Eley**
REPRODUCTION: **Berkeley Square**

Nick Freeth was born in London in 1956, and graduated from St. Catharine's College, Cambridge with a degree in English Literature in 1978. He spent 12 years as a staffer at the BBC World Service, where he specialized in making radio shows covering folk, jazz and blues, and subsequently worked in commercial broadcasting and as a freelance audio producer before becoming a full-time author in 1998. His first two books, co-written with his friend and former colleague Charles Alexander, were *The Acoustic Guitar* and *The Electric Guitar* (both 1999). Nick's more recent output reflects his long-standing fascination with US culture, and includes a history of America in the 1940s, as well as a guide to Route 66, which was published by MBI in 2001.

This edition first published in 2003 by MBI, an imprint of MBI Publishing Company, Galtier Plaza, Suite 200, 380 Jackson Street, St. Paul, MN 55101-3885 USA

© Salamander Books Ltd., 2003

An imprint of **Chrysalis** Books Group plc

MBI titles are also available at discounts in bulk quantity for industrial or sales-promotional use. For details write to Special Sales Manager at Motorbooks International Wholesalers & Distributors, Galtier Plaza, Suite 200, 380 Jackson Street, St. Paul, MN 55101-3885 USA.

ISBN 0-7603-1463-2

PRINTED AND BOUND IN CHINA

CONTENTS

Above: Looking north along Highway 101 from a turnout just beyond Stonefield Beach, Oregon, between the towns of Newport and Florence.

Foreword

A generation or two ago, a huge segment of American society was classed as "Sunday drivers." They even called their vehicles "pleasure cars." Although another huge segment of the population went into fits of a precursor of road rage because these people were much more interested in exploring the landscape than getting out of their way, nearly all of them were beside themselves with joy when a used car dealer told them that a particular creampuff of a car had been formerly owned by a little old lady who only used it on Sundays.

Those days are gone forever, of course. Thanks to the march of progress, few people drive just for the pleasure of it anymore. The goal is to get from point A to point B in the shortest possible amount of time, and the tradeoff has been freeways, turnpikes, interstates and other long ribbons of concrete, often running between high walls so drivers won't be distracted by anything more interesting than the cars around them.

When families attempt over the road excursions, they make it a point to provide the kids with coloring books and other distractions. But in the end, they can usually count on hearing the inevitable whining question, "are we there yet?".

Fortunately, there are still some roads in America where the question rarely comes up, where the family bus can be called a "pleasure car" again, and where, if the question is asked, the answer can be, "We're there right now. And isn't it glorious."

One such combination of roads is the Pacific Coast Highway, stretching for more than 2,000 miles from the top of the Olympic Peninsula to the tip of Baja California. The main highway is what Californians call "the 101," for its designation as the westernmost north-south US route, but there are many places where a high-speed road isn't practical, and in those cases, the road turns inland. The good news is that you don't have to. Highway 1, a narrower, more leisurely road, hugs the shoreline, and it is possible to drive from the State of Washington down to San Diego with views of the Pacific Ocean out of your right-hand window virtually every mile of the way.

But, of course, that isn't all you'll get to enjoy. Far from it. As you'll see in the following pages through the photography of Neil Sutherland. the constantly changing landscape is, if anything, more fascinating than the seascape, itself the most spectacular anywhere in the world. As he and author Nick Freeth took the trip down the highway from Seattle to preview the experience for you, they made it a point to explore some of the other roads just off the beaten path, and what they found there will bring out the explorer in you, too.

The trip is about the joys of nature, from the dramatic mountains up north to the surfers' paradise down at the southern end. It includes the redwood forests, lush farmland and vineyards stretching out as far as the eye can see. It runs past dramatic seaside cliffs, fields strewn with flowers, and bird and wildlife sanctuaries. But is a tour of American history as well. It passes the settlements the Russians hoped would give them the key to this land. It follows the path of the Spaniards who believed it was destined to be theirs forever. And of the Americans who planted their flag in the Golden West and made it stick.

The highway passes near some of America's greatest cities, too. Seattle, Los Angeles, San Diego are among them, and so is San Francisco, reached from the north along the 101 across the Golden Gate Bridge. It touches on some of America's most charming small towns, too, including a few that seem to have been transplanted from the New England coast, and others you'd expect to find in Spain.

The history of the road itself began in 1919, and it was declared open for traffic nineteen years later. The 139-mile stretch from Monterey to Morro Bay was declared California's first scenic highway in 1966, and it is safe to say that it is the most scenic anywhere in America.

Obviously, that stretch of the Pacific Coast Highway is the one to travel if you don't have the time to see all the rest. But the road's joys extend all the way up the coast, and there is enough fascination along the way to provide enough road trips to last a lifetime. At any rate, the memories will.

Above: The harbor at Florence, Oregon provides access to the Siuslaw River.
Opposite page, right: Rocks and sand along the Oregon shore at twilight.

Introduction

Below: Many travelers choose to end their journey down the Pacific Coast Highway with a trip across the Mexican border to the stores, restaurants and bars of Tijuana.

Above: Ancient Egyptian sculptures of the sun goddess Sekhmet, displayed on Hearst Castle's South Esplanade.

Most drivers planning their trip down the Pacific Coast are likely to begin their preparations by consulting a road atlas—and may be somewhat confused by what they see there. The small-scale maps of Washington, Oregon and California, with their colored lines charting the southerly progress of Highways 101 and (later) 1, seem easy enough to follow, but anomalies and uncertainties soon reveal themselves. The 'Pacific Coast Highway' is rarely mentioned by name in modern atlases: what does it actually comprise? There are lengthy stretches, especially in Washington and Oregon, where the main road deviates substantially from the shore: what route should be taken through these areas? Are there sections of the highway that present particular problems to inexperienced or unsuspecting motorists? And what are the PCH's most rewarding natural and man-made sights—aside, of course, from the ever-present ocean, and the National Parks and occasional 'places of interest' indicated on the map? This book attempts to provide comprehensive answers to these key questions, and to give travelers the information they need to make the most of their epic journey from Seattle to Tijuana.

Though the PCH is rightly regarded as one of America's greatest highways, it does not enjoy the same degree of celebrity as Route 66 (the subject of this author's last book for MBI), which, decades after its official decommissioning, still retains its emblematic 'Mother Road' status, attracting many thousands of eager pilgrims each year. Their progress down its 2,000-mile length is eased by clear, consistent signposting, and the numerous roadside motels, stores, diners and even museums bearing the famous '66' logo are constant reminders of its historical and cultural significance. The Pacific Coast Highway does not offer its travelers quite such a clear, well-marked drive. It lacks a uniform system of signs; some of its sections (such as California's Redwood Highway and Cabrillo Highway) have separate identities; and tourists keen to follow it over the contours of the Washington and Oregon shorelines need to be alert for inconspicuous exits, sharp corners, and occasional dead ends as they head for the more isolated coastal communities the road was created to serve.

It is these towns and villages, and the glorious land- and seascapes surrounding them, which give the Highway so much of its distinctive charm. Especially in rural areas, it is an unobtrusive road, causing minimal disruption to the largely unspoiled environment through which it passes. Tourists will want to linger on its most picturesque stretches, and are also likely to be enticed into frequent detours—

Above: Part of the frontage of Hearst Castle's Casa Grande, designed by architect Julia Morgan. The construction of Hearst's hilltop dream home took some 28 years from conception to completion.

along scenic byroads, deep into the forests, parks and wildernesses lying beside and beyond the road, and to nearby sites of interest such as the grave of Willie Keil in Washington State, William Randolph Hearst's 'Enchanted Hill' near San Simeon, California, and—a little to the south and further inland—the tiny settlement of Cholame, where movie star James Dean met his death in 1955.

Succumbing to the temptation of sidetrips somehow seems appropriate to the spirit of the Pacific Coast route. While driving 66 is often seen as

an end in itself, with the highway as the *raison d'être* for the journey, the PCH is essentially a means to an end—a way to reach parts of Washington, Oregon and California that were inaccessible in the years before it was built, and a compelling alternative to the drab monotony of the freeways carrying the heaviest north-south traffic. Its appeal is not only to road 'enthusiasts', but to the rather broader constituency of those fascinated by the rich variety and mystery of America itself. They will not be disappointed by what they find *en route*.

Above: New growths spring from a dead tree trunk lying beside the water in Grays Harbor, Washington, just outside the town of Hoquiam.

What preparations should Pacific Coast Highway travelers make for their journey from Washington to California, and how long will it take them to complete? The first essential is a full tank of gas, which should be regularly replenished; the road has enough lonely, underpopulated stretches to make running out of fuel a major inconvenience, and perhaps even a hazard. The second is a patient, unhurried approach: a considerable proportion of the PCH is narrow and winding, and those prepared to drive it at moderate speed will not only be safer, but have more time to relish its unforgettable qualities. The third is a flexible, even philosophical attitude, especially regarding the weather. Sea mist and indifferent visibility frequently affect parts of the road in Northern California; these murky conditions

Above: Raymond, Washington, and the Willapa River, in about 1905 - an archive photograph from the collection of the Pacific County Historical Society.

Right: Fishing boats and a jetty north of Oregon's Rockaway Beach, on the highway between Seaside and Tillamook.

Left: The sea provides a living for many residents in the more rural areas served by the Pacific Coast Highway: here, a freshly landed oyster is shucked at Brady's, near Westport, WA.

Far left: The towns on Grays Harbor, Washington, owe their existence to fishing and (especially) logging – note the piles of timber near the water.

somehow seem appropriate when visiting locations like the faded old Russian stronghold of Fort Ross *(see pages 86-87)*, but can cause considerable disappointment when they obscure the glories of San Francisco Bay or Mount Tamalpais. If you have the time and inclination to linger in an area of especial interest until skies brighten, so much the better. Farther north, climatic conditions are sometimes less avoidable—one memorable sign at a roadside café near Washington's Hoh Forest proclaims "When you see rain …think of us!"—although early clouds and downpours often dissipate by mid-morning.

This book aims to provide you with full directions from Seattle to Tijuana, but one or more large-scale road maps (like the 1:150,000 series published by DeLorme) would be a useful addition to your glove compartment, particularly when you're planning sidetrips in specific areas. Even with these excellent atlases on board, beware of innocuous looking 'shortcuts', especially from main roads to the shore: they sometimes turn out to be vertiginous, cross-canyon rides! By sticking to the 'prescribed' route, and spending only minimal time in the major cities on your path, it would be possible to complete the entire Washington-Mexico trip in as little as 18 days: however, a longer, more relaxed itinerary is preferable, and will generously replay your greater investment of time.

Above: An exclusive oceanside residence at Pescadero Point, California. This section of the Pacific shoreline is part of the famous '17-mile scenic drive' between Monterey and Carmel.

Washington State

Setting out from Seattle, the city closest to the start of the contiguous Pacific Coast Highway, we explore the Olympic National Park and Forest, and Cape Flattery. We then follow the ocean shore south to Grays Harbor and Willapa Bay—long-established logging centers which contain some of the region's most significant sites of historical interest. The final section of the Washington road leads us to the Long Beach peninsula, and on to the Columbia River crossing into Oregon.

Above and left: Beach logs like these – remnants of mighty trees, left broken and distorted on the shore by the ravages of wind, rain and tide – are a frequent sight along the northwest Pacific coastline.

WASHINGTON STATE

| Seattle | | Bremerton | | Crocker Lake | 0094 | La Poel |
| 0000 | Puget Sound | 0019 | Hood Canal | 0058 | Port Angeles | 0117 |

Washington State

Above: The Territory of Washington's seal, bearing the Chinook word 'Alki' ('By and By') - later the state motto.

Many of the coastal features of what is now Washington State were named by (or for) the seafarers who were its earliest European visitors. Apostolos Valerianos, a Greek also known as Juan de Fuca, claimed to have sailed the north-western Pacific in 1592—though the position of the "Strait of Juan de Fuca" he is said to have discovered was not accurately determined until two centuries after his alleged voyage. By then, the great age of exploration by ship was under way, and the English navigators Captains James Cook and George Vancouver both added substantially to the once inadequate maps of the region. Another British seaman, John Meares, also made his mark here—trading with local Indian tribes (who responded to his double-dealing by dubbing him "Aitaaita"—"the liar") and naming Mount Olympus, now at the heart of the Olympic National Park. On first seeing it in 1788, he exclaimed, "If that be not the home where dwell the Gods, it is beautiful enough to be."

The 1790s and 1800s saw Britain's territorial ambitions in the Pacific northwest being increasingly countered by America. In 1792, Captain Robert Gray claimed Grays Harbor and the Columbia river for the nation; and in November 1805, the U.S. Corps of Volunteers for Northwest Discovery, led by Meriwether Lewis and William Clark, arrived at the mouth of the Columbia after a 16-month journey from the Missouri River. These men's achievements strengthened the conviction among their contemporaries that, as historian Hugh Brogan puts it, "the United States would one day stretch from the Atlantic to the Pacific." However, America did not gain exclusive jurisdiction over the northwest until the signature of the Oregon Treaty with Britain in

Right: Some sections of Washington State's shoreline have been subjected to substantial erosion from the tides.

Below: One of a series of bumper stickers with memorably salty slogans produced by Brady's Oysters of Westport, Washington.

Cranberry Museum
FURFORD Mfg.Co.
FURFORD PICKERS
CLOSED   TOURS 267 - 5403

Above and far right: The town of Grayland owes its prosperity to cranberries; its museum is devoted to the history of their cultivation.

"Nothing in Life Prep for Your First Raw

Right: These photographs of a Columbia River salmon cannery and a local oyster boat date from the early 1900s.

0139 — Sappho
Clallam Bay — 0156
0159 — Sekiu
Neah Bay — 0177
0185 — Cape Flattery
Beaver — 0235
0243 — Forks
Ruby Beach — 0274

1846. Seven years later, Congress established a "Washington Territory" separate from the "Oregon Country," and in 1889, the region achieved statehood.

Settlers had been attracted to Washington by its fertile lands and abundant natural resources; they exploited and profited from these, but have also been keen to preserve and share them with visitors. In 1897, President Grover Cleveland endorsed the creation of the Olympic Forest Reserve; which became a National Park in 1938. Access to it is easy, thanks to the proximity of Route 101—but not all of Washington's western shoreline is so accessible, and drivers need to be alert for turnoffs and cul-de-sacs when seeking out its beaches, bays and peninsulas. Their persistence will be richly rewarded, as this area offers some of the most unique and striking scenery to be found anywhere on the Pacific Coast Highway.

Above: The North Head lighthouse, located on the western tip of the Long Beach peninsula.
Left: A mural on the side of a store in Raymond depicts logging on Willapa Bay.

WASHINGTON STATE

Seattle		Bremerton		Crocker Lake		0094		La Poel

0000   *Puget Sound*   0019   *Hood Canal*   0058   Port Angeles   0117

Olympic Park/Hurricane Ridge

Bottom left: The harbor at Sekiu, on Washington State's north coast.
Below: Looking along the shore at Cape Flattery. Over $200,000 has recently been spent in improving access to the Cape, and visitors can enjoy scenes like this from newly-constructed walkways and observation decks.

To reach the Olympic Peninsula, take the ferry from Seattle's Pier 52 across the Puget Sound to Bremerton, and drive north on Highway 3. About four miles past the little town of Breidablick, turn northwest onto Highway 104, cross the Hood Canal, and continue to Crocker Lake, 14 miles further on.

Beyond the Lake, we join Highway 101 as it approaches the perimeter of the vast Olympic

National Park and Forest that form the heart of the peninsula. After skirting Sequim, with its roadside fruit- and lavender-fields, 101 heads for Port Angeles, the region's largest settlement; the exit for the Park HQ and Visitor Center lies just within its city limits. This turnoff also leads to one of the Park's most popular attractions, Hurricane Ridge, which is especially rich in flora and fauna. The Ridge's vista point, 5,242 feet above sea level, can provide spectacular views of nearby mountains and sea—though visibility is often adversely affected by the Peninsula's famously misty, rainy climate!

The Hurricane Ridge road is a dead end; we resume our journey by returning to 101. The highway stays close to the Park and Forest as it continues west, passing Lake Crescent and crossing

the Sol Duc River on its way to Sappho. Here, we turn north towards the coast—first on Route 113, and then on 112, which brings us to the fishing village of Clallam Bay before following the shoreline to Sekiu and the boundary of the Makah Indian Reservation at Neah Bay.

A Makah Nation "recreational use" permit (currently costing $7, and available at stores and businesses in Neah Bay) should be purchased before driving the last 8 miles to Cape Flattery. The "Cape Trail" is roughly surfaced in places, and its final stretch can only be accessed on foot. However, the unforgettable view at its end—taking in the land's edge and ocean, and accompanied by the boom of the waves breaking inside the caves beneath the Cape—amply justifies the long journey needed to get there.

Above: A deer glimpsed by the roadside at Hurricane Ridge. A wide range of other animals and birds make this area their home – but are frequently shy of cars and cameras.

Above right and top right: Captain James Cook pictured in London shortly before setting out on his third and final voyage of exploration to the Pacific in 1776; and the view northwest from Cape Flattery (discovered and named by Cook in 1778) to Tatoosh Island, which lies about half a mile offshore.

Cape Flattery

Cape Flattery was given its name by the English navigator Captain James Cook (1728-1779), who sailed up the coast of what was then known as 'New Albion' from Oregon to Washington in March 1778. In his journal, Cook records that, on March 22, he sighted "a small opining in the land which flatered us with hopes of finding a harbour. These hopes lessened as we drew nearer, and at last we had some reason to think that this opining was closed by lowland. On this account I called the point of land to the North of it Cape Flatery…"
Cook had come to the American continent (via Australasia and Hawaii) with instructions from the British Admiralty to seek out "a Northern passage by Sea from the Pacific to the Atlantic Ocean." This eluded him (it was successfully navigated by Roald Amundsen in 1903-6), and bad weather ("a very hard gale with rain right on shore") also prevented him from locating the Strait of Juan de Fuca—the inlet, north of Cape Flattery, between Washington and Vancouver Island.

The Hoh Rain Forest

Below (left and right): Trees like the one below, seen on the Hoh Forest's 'Hall of Mosses' trail, are unharmed by the beards of fern and lichen festooning their branches. Forest plantlife thrives on the warm, damp climate, which is sustained by airborne moisture as well as by streams and ground water.

As there is no coastal road south from Cape Flattery, we must now double back through Neah Bay, Sekiu and Clallam Bay, and continue on 101 from the point where we left it at Sappho. Soon, the highway turns south through the Sol Duc Valley; the Olympic National Forest can be seen to the left, and, 13 miles beyond Forks, is the turnoff for one of the peninsula's most remarkable natural phenomena: the Hoh Rain Forest.

While Forks has the distinction of being Washington State's wettest town, with an annual rainfall of over 113 inches in 2001, the Hoh Forest receives even more precipitation—"an average of 140 inches a year... and that's not counting the fog," according to park service volunteer Jerry Morris in a recent *Seattle Post-Intelligencer* article. This microclimate, the result of the nearby Olympic Mountains causing currents of warm air to rise and

Right, and far right: Sunlight breaks through the Hoh's canopy of leaves and tree limbs, illuminating a dense profusion of growth. The forest floor is so crowded with vegetation that the roots of younger trees frequently become entwined with fragments of fallen, decaying trunks.

release their moisture, creates ideal conditions for the countless plant species that flourish in the forest. Spruce, maple and cedar grow hundreds of feet high; mosses and ferns drape themselves over the trunks and branches of living trees; and even dead and rotting timbers support new vegetation, serving as "nurselogs" for freshly sprouting flora. There is also an abundance of animal life—both at

Above: Even this phone booth, adjacent to the Forest's Visitor Center, has attracted its own 'thatch' of moss!

ground level, where elk graze among the trees, and far above, where birds and flying squirrels nest and feed in the canopies of leaves.

To explore the Rain Forest, drive the 18 miles from the Highway 101 exit to the Visitor Center. This is the starting point for a number of well-signposted walking trails—including the ¾-mile "Hall of Mosses" trail, which provides an excellent introduction to the area's unique environment. For the more adventurous, there are longer treks (such as a 36-mile round trip to the Blue Glacier on Mount Olympus), as well as opportunities for riding, canoeing and camping.

WASHINGTON STATE

Crocker Lake | 0094 | La Poel | 0139 | Clallam Bay | 0159 | Neah Bay
0058 | Port Angeles | 0117 | Sappho | 0156 | Sekiu | 0177

Right: The view north along Ruby Beach, showing its stony, wood-strewn foreshore. Many of the logs are fallen tree trunks torn from the surrounding forest by fierce winter storms.

For much of its length, the side road leading to and from the Rain Forest is flanked by the Hoh River. Fast flowing and rich in fish, the Hoh (named, like the forest, for a local Indian tribe) rises on Mount Olympus, some 7,000 feet above sea level; south of the Forest exit, it continues close to 101 as highway and river both make their way to the ocean.

A couple of miles from the shore, 101 diverges from the Hoh, turning south and giving us, for the first time on our journey, the opportunity to drive beside the Pacific, and explore its beaches. The coast here is part of a 3,300 square mile National Marine Sanctuary, set up in 1994, and extending from near Cape Flattery south to Copalis. Among its most striking features are the beach logs, sometimes bizarrely twisted by wind and waves, that litter the sand. These include fragments of rain forest trees, as well as trunks and branches blown down from nearby headlands. At Ruby Beach, the first of a chain of beaches we encounter on a 14-mile stretch of 101 in this area, accumulated driftwood near the

tidemark forms a barrier that visitors must scramble over to reach the water. However, its presence also serves a valuable ecological purpose, helping to protect the fragile coastline from erosion.

Above: The Big Cedar, sited just off the stretch of Pacific coast between Ruby Beach and Kalaloch. Its massive, twisted trunk stands out from the tall but slender trees that surround it, and dwarfs the human figure to its right.

Right: Looking southeast from the Rain Forest Visitor Center road across the Hoh River, whose waters, yielding salmon, steelhead, and other fish species, are a major attraction for anglers.

Along the shore are tidal pools containing crustaceans and other tiny creatures; mammals such as seals and sea lions also thrive here, while migrating whales can sometimes be spotted out to sea. And, about 2 miles south of Ruby Beach, a path from an off-road parking area leads to one of the most widely photographed trees on our route: the famous "Big Cedar" (occasionally called the "Kalaloch Cedar"). It stands 123 feet high, and is among the largest specimens of *Thuja plicata* in Washington State, although there are a few taller cedars to be found within the Olympic National Forest and near the Hoh River.

Above: Rising tide at Ruby Beach. The protruding rock formations in the water are 'seastacks', created by ancient volcanic eruptions, Abbey Island stands a few yards offshore.

Below: The view along the shore at Taholah. The settlement lies at the mouth of the Quinault River, just south of Cape Elizabeth; there is no passable road north from here.

Above: The low cliffs at Ocean Beach (located a few miles down the coast from Taholah, between Pacific and Copalis Beaches) seen from sea level.

Right: An aerial shot of the logging pens in the waters of Grays Harbor near Hoquiam. Appropriately, the town's name is derived from an Amerindian word meaning 'hungry for wood'; many of its past residents have made their fortunes from timber.

The most impressive of the roadside beaches south of the Big Cedar is at Kalaloch, about five miles down the coast; it boasts an enticingly wide expanse of sand, though its unpredictable tides make bathing hazardous. Beyond it, Highway 101 enters the Quinault Indian Reservation, and bends away from the shore, passing Quinault Lake, and the towns of Amanda Park and Neilton.

Five miles south of Neilton, we leave 101, and head southwest on Route 109. This brings us back to the sea at Moclips, a popular holiday destination in the days when the Northern Pacific Railroad connected it with Seattle, and the location for John Wayne's 1974 movie *McQ*. We continue up the coast to Taholah, where 109 deadends. The town is the headquarters of the Quinault Nation, and the base for their thriving commercial fishing activities; it can also be considered the true start of the Pacific

Above: The American seafarer Captain Robert Gray, who gave his name to Grays Harbor.

Coast Highway, which runs almost unbroken from here to southern California.

We now double back, following 109 south to the mouth of Grays Harbor; here, the road turns east towards Hoquiam. The harbor was named for Captain Robert Gray (1755–1806), who, in 1792, became the first white American to sail into it. Hoquiam, a long-established center for the lumber trade, contains a number of notable houses created by its wealthy residents. These include the Polson Mansion, built by sawmill owner Robert Polson in 1924, and Hoquiam's Castle—the former home of timber baron Robert Lytle, dating from 1897 and now a luxurious bed-and-breakfast inn. A few miles east on 109 lies Aberdeen, a larger logging town that was the childhood home of rock musician Kurt Cobain (1967-1994), leader of Nirvana. Cobain has no prominent memorial there—though other

| 0375 | Ocean City | 0396 | Aberdeen | 0414 | Westport | 0447 | Tokeland |
| Copalis Beach | 0378 | Hoquiam | 0400 | Markham | 0424 | Grayland | 0455 |

Cosmopolis

Above: One of a series of colorful murals by local artist Dick Creevan adorning stores in downtown Aberdeen.
Right: The road bridge carrying Highway 101 south across Grays Harbor from Aberdeen toward Cosmopolis.

aspects of Aberdeen's heritage are preserved in its harbor and Museum of History.

Before leaving this area, take a short detour south down Highway 101 to Cosmopolis, where a plaque and mural mark the site of talks in 1855 between government officials and Native Americans that led to a treaty with the Quinault and Quillaute tribes.

> " At the northern end of this timber country the land and the sea become inextricably mixed, and the map is a mass of small blue streaks, patches, and fingers, where the inlets and lagoons of the Pacific eat their way into Washington state. "

Jan Morris, Northwest Extremity, *from Coast to Coast (1956)*

Above: Another Dick Creevan mural (this one was created in 1987, in collaboration with his wife, Lynn). It stands at 1st and H Streets in Cosmopolis to commemorate the U.S.-Native American treaty of 1855.

Agriculture

Below and centre right: Logging trucks carry freshly-hewn timber from its areas of cultivation to the sawmill. Our archive photo shows Washington timberers at work in about 1908.

Forests dominate the landscape for the early part of our trip, and remain a constant factor for much of the rest of its length. They are also vital to the economic life of the states we pass through; for several years, Oregon has been the largest producer of lumber in the US, with Washington and California not far behind. However, the days when, in the words of one historian of the logging industry, "timber was effectively there for the taking" are long gone. Felling on federal land is now strictly limited (accounting for less than 10% of wood harvested in the Pacific Northwest), and the "jobs grow with trees" signs often seen near roadside woodlands also list the numbers of new saplings being planted to replace the ones cut down.

Other agriculture along the highway has developed through a combination of perfect

environment and personal enterprise. In the 1880s, cranberry vines were first planted on boggy land near Washington's Long Beach. Cultivation quickly spread to other parts of the state, and in the 1940s, growers "dry-harvesting" their berries by hand had their backbreaking work in the fields eased by the invention of a simple but effective picker/pruner machine by Grayland resident Julius Furford, which is now in use throughout the world.

Unsurprisingly, the "Ocean Spray" cranberry juice logo is a frequent sight in Washington; but across the state line in Oregon, mentions for "Tillamook Cheese" start to grow in frequency. Surrounded by rich grazing pastures, Tillamook has been a significant center for dairy produce since the first cheese factory was opened there in 1894 by T. F. Townsend, a butter maker from the town. Today, the Tillamook Cheese co-operative is among the area's biggest businesses; its Visitor Center, on Highway 101 just north of the town, offers self-guided tours and a chance to sample locally made cheddar and ice cream.

California's windswept headlands seem less suited for livestock than the lush fields of Tillamook, though some hardy cattle flourish on the steep slopes adjacent to the highway north of San Francisco. Further south, a more intensive form of Golden State agriculture can be seen alongside Highway 1: the dusty fields in this region produce huge yields of salad crops and strawberries, and employ substantial teams of laborers—often Mexicans—to tend and reap them.

Above: Farmworkers near Guadalupe, CA purify the soil in their fields with methane gas, prior to planting strawberries.
Left: Dairy cattle in the roadside meadows beside the Ocean Spit/Cape Meares road, just south of Tillamook, OR.

Top and center left: A mural in Long Beach, WA depicts a 1920 cranberry harvest. Today's growers have their lives made easier by the Furford picker/pruner.

WASHINGTON STATE

0375 Copalis Beach
Ocean City
0378
0396 Hoquiam
Aberdeen
0400
0414 Markham
Westport
0424
0447 Grayland

Right: A fresh catch of oysters at Brady's outside Westport.
Far right: The town's Marina – a favorite with locals and tourists.

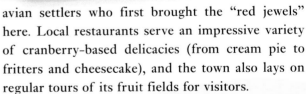

Above: Grayland's Community Hall – built in 1930 by local residents, it is appropriately cranberry-colored, and sited on the town's Cranberry Road.

Below: The little town of Tokeland lies at the tip of a small peninsula near the mouth of Willapa Bay.

Grays Harbor is a v-shaped inlet, and Aberdeen lies almost at its narrowest point. After passing through the city, we take Route 105, which leads along the harbor's southern edge, through Markham, and over the Elk River Bridge towards Westport. Just offshore here are oyster beds belonging to Brady's, a seafood company whose jetty, processing plant and small retail store can be seen, to the right of the road, on the far side of the bridge.

To reach the Westport peninsula, we continue for another mile or so before turning north onto Forrest Street. Our first port of call in town is the 107-foot Grays Harbor lighthouse on Ocean Avenue (left off Forrest); it dates from 1898, and is still in use. Further up Forrest is the approach to the popular Marina area, with shops, restaurants, and, on Westhaven Drive, a Maritime Museum housed in an elegant former coastguard station. A few yards away, this little spur of land ends, and we double back to resume our journey south.

Grayland, the next settlement on 105, is at the center of one of Washington's major cranberry-growing regions, and many of its residents are descended from the nineteenth century Scandin-

avian settlers who first brought the "red jewels" here. Local restaurants serve an impressive variety of cranberry-based delicacies (from cream pie to fritters and cheesecake), and the town also lays on regular tours of its fruit fields for visitors.

105 now follows the coastline as it bends east past Cape Shoalwater and "Washaway Beach." For the past century, the sea has been dramatically eroding the land here, and some 120 feet of sand are continuing to vanish every year. Just beyond Washaway is Tokeland, named for the Shoalwater Indian Chief Toke. The nearby Tokeland Hotel, a favorite with high society guests in the pre-Depression years, retains its old-world charm—though the private golfing and shooting facilities it once offered its patrons are now gone. From Tokeland, it is a 12-mile journey into the mouth of Willapa Bay to Raymond.

Above: Vacationers enjoying themselves on Tokeland Beach - a photograph taken in 1912.
Below: 'Washaway Beach' marks the southern edge of Washington's so-called 'Cranberry Coast'.

Below: A freshly-landed catch of gill-netted king salmon on the quay at South Bend. The surrounding sea is also renowned for its oysters and crab.

Below: The Willapa River and the region around the town of Raymond seen from the air – like Grays Harbor, this area is a significant center for lumber processing and transportation.

A friendly, unpretentious place, Raymond earns much of its livelihood from logging, and celebrates the industry with numerous murals and statues on its streets. However, the little town has several other interesting features—including an elegant municipal theatre, built in 1928 and equipped with a vintage Wurlitzer organ. Raymond is also investing in the future; its central area has recently undergone a two million-dollar refurbishment, and further expansion and improvement is continuing near its Alder Street riverfront.

The next stage of our journey will take us south from here along the shores of Willapa Bay. First, though, we make a sidetrip inland to a place with a strange and haunting story associated with it: the grave of Willie Keil (1836-1855), a would-be migrant from Missouri who died before he could start his journey west, and whose body was carried on a wagon train and buried at the place where he had hoped to settle. Willie's grave, in an old hilltop cemetery on Route 6 about 7 miles east of Raymond, is not very easily accessible; but a Washington State Parks Historic Marker has been placed nearby to commemorate him.

Above, left and right: Raymond, present and past... Its theatre, at 323 3rd Street, was opened in 1928, about twenty years after the severe flooding depicted in the old Pacific County Historical Society photo of the town.

Above top: A busy jetty at South Bend harbor. The town, four miles from Raymond, took over from Oysterville as the local County Seat in 1893.

Tokeland

0476

South Bend

0522

Oysterville

0554

Chinook

0455

Raymond

0480

Long Beach

0536

Ilwaco

0562

Columbia River

Willie Keil's Grave

Willie Keil

Willie Keil's father, Dr. William Keil, was the leader of the Bethelite religious sect, made up of German emigrants and taking its name from the town of Bethel, Missouri, where they had settled in 1844. Eleven years later, Dr. Keil determined to take his followers west to a new home on the Pacific coast. Willie was enthusiastic about the move, and asked to be allowed to drive the group's lead wagon—but four days before their departure in May 1855, he was stricken with a fever and died. Dr. Keil honored his son's wish to travel with the group, placing his body in a whiskey-filled, lead-lined coffin, and transporting it, at the head of the Bethelite wagon train, from Missouri to the Willapa Valley, where Willie was laid to rest on November 26, 1855.

After visiting this site, we return to Raymond and follow Route 101 to South Bend, the self-styled "Oyster Capital of the World" and "Baltimore of the Pacific." Among its many attractions is an outstanding architectural asset—the beautiful County Courthouse on Memorial Drive, built at a cost of $132,000 in 1910–11. Early critics dubbed the Courthouse "the gilded palace of extravagance,"

but public opinion soon turned in its favor, and it was made a Registered National Historic Place in 1977. Despite its opulent appearance, the Courthouse's interior is not quite all it seems; its "marble" columns are actually plain cement, skillfully camouflaged with paint by a prisoner from the local County jail in the 1940s!

Above (in box): The burial place of Willie Keil. This disused graveyard lies in the fields above Willie's memorial marker on Route 6; it should not be confused with the modern cemetery a little farther along the highway, which has no connection with the Bethelites.

Above: Looking south down Long Beach's main drag, Pacific Avenue (Highway 103), from 3rd Street.
Below: Oysterville's original Baptist Church, located at the south edge of town. It was built by the community's co-founder, R. H. Espy, in 1892, and is still used for services every Summer.

Photo by Wayne O'Neil

Right: The mooring basin at Nahcotta, on the Peninsula's eastern coast, a few miles below Oysterville. Nearby attractions include the Willapa Bay Interpretive Center, opened in 1993.

On leaving South Bend, 101 rarely strays far from the water's edge until it nears the southern end of Willapa Bay. Here, the highway bears west, and soon reaches a junction with Route 103—the road we now take north to explore the Long Beach Peninsula.

Curiously, the first town to be established on this thin finger of land lies not immediately ahead of us, but at a location some 14 miles away, to which, in 1854, two young entrepreneurs were attracted by an abundance of offshore oysters. The pair, Robert H. Espy and I. A. Clark, founded Oysterville there, and within a year it had grown sufficiently in size and wealth to be made the surrounding region's county seat—a position it eventually lost to South Bend in 1893. By this time, oyster yields were dropping, and

the town's glory days were gone. However, it remains a charming, atmospheric place, whose special character has been captured in a best-selling book by Robert Espy's grandson, Willard, entitled *Oysterville, Roads to Grandpa's Village.*

Individual enterprise was also the driving force behind the creation of the Peninsula's two other main settlements. Ex-Oysterville resident Jonathon L. Stout built Seaview, where 101 now meets 103, in 1881; at about the same time, Henry Harrison Tinker was laying out "Tinkerville" (subsequently renamed Long Beach) just to the north. Both developments had excellent hotel and camping facilities, and proved massively popular with visitors—who arrived by stagecoach and steamship from Oregon, and were soon able to travel up the

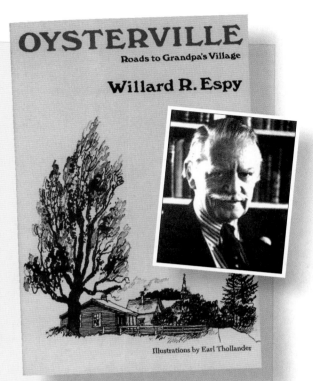

> " Imagine it is the fall of 1855. You are a passenger aboard a three-masted, hundred-ton schooner that has been clawing its way north from San Francisco for the past two and a half weeks. [...] Westward, five miles away, is the North Beach peninsula; the first mate's glass enables you to pick out the scattering of cabins that make up the new settlement of Oysterville... If you could take flight, as swans and seagulls are doing all about you, you would see that the peninsula behind the village is scarcely a mile wide, with a central spine no more than fifty feet high. Its western slope descends to swamps and lakes; these in turn press against the great inner dune that marks the beginning of the ocean beach. "

Willard R. Espy, Oysterville – Roads to Grandpa's Village, *1977*

Peninsula on the narrow-gauge "Clamshell Railroad" that opened in 1888, and was to serve the area until 1930.

Today, Seaview and Long Beach are colorful, bustling modern resorts with little to remind us of their past, and 103 has replaced both the train and the old plank and dirt roads that Stout and Tinker would have known. The adjacent beaches, though, are as impressive as ever, and the boardwalk running north from Long Beach's South 10th Street is one "tourist attraction" that should not be missed.

Right: *North Head and its lighthouse from the south (a closer view of the light appears on page 17). In the foreground are the western shores of Fort Canby State Park; Long Beach stretches away beyond the Head.*

WASHINGTON
STATE

| 0375 | Ocean City | 0396 | Aberdeen | 0414 | Westport | 0447 |
Copalis Beach | 0378 | Hoquiam | 0400 | Markham | 0424 | Grayland

Below: State-wide programs and information schemes are in place to counteract the potential dangers of tsunamis - giant waves caused by underwater earthquakes.

TSUNAMI EVACUATION ROUTE

Right: Wild sweet peas growing beside the highway on the outskirts of Raymond. Washington's mild, rainy climate supports an abundance of plant life; the state is home to some 270 native species of wildflower.

From Seaview, the southern end of the Long Beach Peninsula can be reached by turning left on 101 and heading for Ilwaco, about 2 miles away. The town—called Unity by Civil War soldiers billeted at nearby Fort Canby, but renamed in 1873 for Elowahka, the daughter of a local Indian chief—is a significant fishing port, and the gateway to several other sites of historical interest.

Among these is the Fort Canby State Park, a few miles to the southwest. It includes an Interpretive Center devoted to the achievements and discoveries of Meriwether Lewis and William Clark *(see pages 42-43)*, sited close to the spot where the two great explorers first looked out over Cape Disappointment in November 1805. The Cape, described in Clark's journal as "an ellivated circular point... ris[ing] with a Steep assent to the hight of about 150 or 160 feet above the leavel of the water," was christened by the English seafarer John Meares, who, in 1788, had been unable to find a passage into the adjacent Columbia River. Its mouth and the surrounding coastline are among the most hazardous places on the Pacific seaboard, and since the nineteenth century, ships in the region have been safeguarded by two lighthouses. One was built at Cape Disappointment itself in 1856, and the other, dating from 1898, lies west of Ilwaco at North Head: both are open to visitors.

101 now continues east on the final stretch of its route through Washington State. Beyond Chinook, the road passes through a short tunnel, and runs close to the water as it approaches the majestic Astoria-Megler bridge over the Columbia. This was opened in August 1966; prior to its construction, interstate traffic had had to rely on a car ferry from Megler, just east of where the bridge leaves the Washington shore. The ferry took over half an hour to get to Astoria, but we make the crossing in minutes; half way along its four-mile length is the sign welcoming us to Oregon.

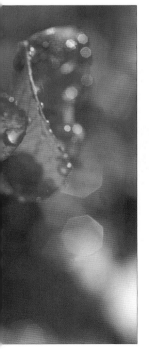

Above: The Washington bank of the Columbia River, and the Astoria-Megler bridge to Oregon, seen from beside Highway 101. At 4.1 miles, the Astoria-Megler is the longest continuous truss-type bridge in North America; it is toll-free, and carries several thousand vehicles each day.

Left: The lighthouse and cliffs at Cape Disappointment. After navigating around them, ships headed for the mouth of the Columbia River and the port of Astoria face other formidable navigational obstacles, including a dangerous sandbar.

Oregon

Oregon's coastline stretches for over 350 miles from Astoria to just beyond Brookings. Except for Coos Bay and its neighbor, North Bend, there are no especially large urban areas here, and our route is dominated by a dramatic, constantly varying succession of headlands and shores. Many of these can be seen without leaving Highway 101, although we take occasional detours from the main road to visit some more isolated beauty spots— including a few of the capes and beaches seen and named by this region's first explorers and settlers.

Above: Sunset, shadows and seastacks on the shores of Oregon. Even the Beaver State's wildest and loneliest beaches are relatively easily to reach from the Pacific Coast Highway.

Oregon

Pacific Coast Scenic Byway

Above: Signs like these help to keep the traveler on track in Oregon.
Below: A sand sculptor creates an impressive, though sadly short-lived artwork on the beach at Seaside.

Numerous eighteenth-century navigators surveyed the coastline around Cape Disappointment, but an American, Captain Robert Gray, was the first of them to sail into the natural harbor just beyond it. This historic event took place in May 1792, when Gray, en route from his previous anchorage in Grays Harbor (see pages 24–25), succeeded in finding a safe passage between the treacherous sand-bars near the cape, and toward the mouth of what he believed to be a major inland waterway. On May 11, he entered the river, christening it the Columbia (for his ship, the *Columbia Rediviva*), and establishing America's claim to the surrounding area. The Columbia's significance was confirmed after Lewis and Clark traveled down it in 1805. They went on to spend several months near its banks, and the best-selling account of their journey, first

published in 1814, played a key role in stimulating later, large-scale westward migration. The "Oregon Territory" ("Ourigon" was the name given to a supposed "Great River of the West" by early geographers) was formally established in 1848, and statehood followed eleven years later.

Reaching the region was far from easy for the first settlers. The overland Oregon Trail from Missouri led across harsh terrain, some of it occupied by hostile tribes; while for those arriving by sea, the quotation from a famous religious poem by Alfred, Lord Tennyson, "I hope to see my Pilot face to face/When I have crossed the bar", displayed inside the Cape Disappointment lighthouse, had a starkly literal meaning. On a more lighthearted note, it has been suggested that adverse conditions on the Columbia may have led to the creation of the Tillamook

Right: The Tillamook Cheese logo. This farmers' cooperative has been in business since 1909.

Right: On the Cape Blanco River Trail, northwest of Port Orford – a bracing, windswept walk from the highway to the ocean, through fields dotted with rocks and ruined trees.

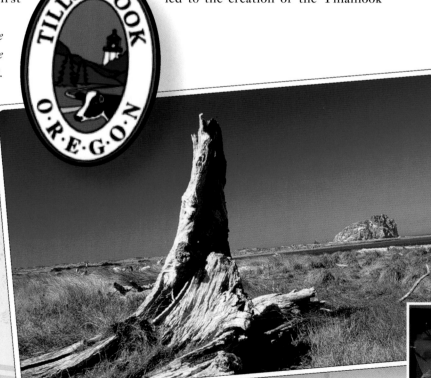

TILLAMOOK
O·R·E·G·O·N

Right: Storefront decorations in the Old Town neighborhood of Florence.

cheese industry, after delays in putting to sea caused cargoes of butter to turn rancid!

The arrival of railroads improved access to Oregon; however, it was progress in highway construction that did most to boost business and tourism. In 1913, Governor Oswald West became the first chairman of the State Highway Commission, which initiated an energetic program of road development. Within a decade, the entire length of the Pacific Highway through Oregon (later named Route 101) had been paved, although a number of bridges were still unfinished; work on 101 was finally completed in 1941. West, who served as Governor from 1911 to 1915, is also remembered for passing the Oswald West Act of 1913 – an ingenious piece of legislation that declared all Oregon's beaches and tidelands to be public highways, making it impossible for them to be sold off for commercial gain.

Above: Looking north up the coast from near Tolovana State Park, a beauty spot just south of Cannon Beach. Haystack Rock (see pages 44-5) is visible in the bay, though partially obscured by tree branches.

Below: The view across the busy Columbia River from the Area D beach at Fort Stevens State Park, a few miles beyond Astoria.

Below: Rogue River jet boats, featured on p.66.

MAIL BOAT HYDRO-JET TRIPS

Above: Former Oregon Governor Oswald West (1873-1960).

Above: The scene from the South Jetty viewing platform in Area C of the Fort Stevens State Park. Approximately 10 miles from Astoria, the Park covers over 3,500 acres.

Above top: The elegant and distinctive Astoria Column – which also provides a superb view of the surrounding region for visitors energetic enough to climb the 164 steps to its observation deck.

Some state boundaries pass by almost unnoticed, but arriving in Oregon and encountering Astoria triggers an immediate shift in most travelers' moods. Though a small city (with a population of just over 10,000), it has a sophisticated, cosmopolitan atmosphere that is in marked contrast to the simpler charms of many towns in Washington—and, with its hilly location and Victorian architecture, is sometimes described as "the little San Francisco of the northwest."

Astoria took its name from John Jacob Astor (1763-1848), the German-born fur trader who built a stockade here in 1811. It soon established itself as a significant port and a center for logging and fishing, and became the western terminus for the Astoria and Columbia River Railroad (later part of the Great Northern Railway) in 1898. It was the Great Northern's President, Ralph Budd, who was largely responsible for the creation of the city's best-known and most prominent monument, the 125-foot Astoria Column, in 1926. Designed by New York architect Electus Litchfield, and inspired by the Emperor Trajan's column in Rome, it is decorated with a frieze depicting fourteen key events in the development of the Astoria region. Among these are Robert Gray's entry into the mouth of the Columbia, the Lewis and Clark expedition, the construction of John Jacob Astor's fort, and the coming of the railroad.

The column stands on the city's Coxcomb Hill, a position that provides impressive views of the surrounding area, including the Astoria-Megler bridge stretching back to Washington, and the shorter Warrenton bridge that carries Highway 101 over Young's Bay and on down the coast. This is the route we take to continue our journey—though just after crossing the Warrenton bridge, it is well worth turning right onto Harbor Street and heading for the Fort Stevens State Park near Hammond. A major defense site from the Civil War period until the end of World War II, the park contains gun batteries and other artifacts, and (on a clear day) provides a final, spectacular glimpse of the Columbia River.

Above: Looking back across the four-mile stretch of water to Washington State from the Astoria bank of the Columbia River.

Left: An aerial photograph of the Astoria area, taken from the west. The Astoria–Megler bridge (also shown in the picture above) can be seen near the top left of this shot.

Right: The distinctive 'sgraffito' frieze decorating the outside of the Astoria Column is the work of Italian-born artist Attilio Pusterla (1862–1941).

STATE OF OREGON
1859
OREGON

| Astoria | 0573 | Hammond | 0588 | Cannon Beach | 0608 | Nehalem |
| 0571 | Warrenton | 0578 | Seaside | 0594 | Manzanita | 0610 |

Below: Seaside has important associations with Lewis and Clark – though their journey continued some miles beyond the site of the town.

From the River View Point in the Fort Stevens State Park, it is possible to return to 101 via Lake Drive, Ridge Road and Columbia Beach Road. However, we now rejoin it using the Fort Stevens Highway/Harbor Street route on which we entered the Park, and continue south along the highway for a short distance before taking the exit leading to the Fort Clatsop National Memorial.

This was the site where the Lewis and Clark expedition spent the winter of 1805-6. The reconstructed "fort"—two log cabins with a wooden stockade fence at either end—is based on the original "fourtification" completed by the men on January 1, 1806. In his journal, Lewis records that they celebrated New Year there by letting off a volley of small arms fire, before partaking of a dreary meal of boiled elk. Nothing remains of the original buildings, but the replicas are realistically furnished, and there are regular demonstrations and exhibitions to convey the often harsh reality of life in the garrison.

Resuming our journey on 101, we head for another location with important links to Lewis and Clark. In 1805, a group from Fort Clatsop set up a camp close to the ocean some 15 miles southwest of their stockade, where they extracted salt crystals (needed to preserve their food) from the seawater. Decades later, the same area came to the attention of another visitor: Kentucky-born entrepreneur Ben Holliday (1819-1887), a millionaire stagecoach owner and railroad developer who established a fashionable resort there in the 1870s. He named it Seaside, and its wide, sandy beach has been attracting locals and vacationers ever since. The town has not forgotten its connection with the explorers: a replica of their salt works can be seen

The Lewis and Clark Expedition

In 1803, President Thomas Jefferson commissioned an expedition to explore the course of the Missouri River and find a route from its source to the Pacific Ocean. He placed two army officers, Captain Meriwether Lewis and Lieutenant William Clark, in charge of it, and they set off, with a small accompanying party, from near St. Louis, Missouri on May 14, 1804. Their trip northwest, by boat and on foot, took them through regions about which little or nothing was known; as instructed by the President, they surveyed them, and kept detailed records of the natives, plants and wildlife they encountered. After heading up the Missouri and crossing the Rockies and Bitterroot Mountains, they found navigable rivers that eventually brought them to the sea in November 1805. They started for home the following March, and were back in Missouri by September 1806, having covered a total of over 6,000 miles.

Right: The memorial erected to Meriwether Lewis and William Clark at the top of Seaside's Broadway – the street that leads west to the town's popular beach.

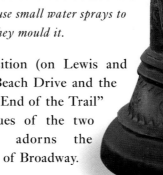

Near and far right and above right: Sand sculpting is a popular activity at Seaside, and many of the artists at work on the beach here are professionals. They use small water sprays to keep the sand moist as they mould it.

near its original position (on Lewis and Clark Way between Beach Drive and the Promenade); and an "End of the Trail" memorial, with statues of the two expedition leaders, adorns the turnaround at the top of Broadway.

STATE OF OREGON
1859
OREGON

0588 · Seaside
Cannon Beach · 0594
0608 · Manzanita
Nehalem · 0610
0613 · Wheeler
Rockaway Beach · 0617
0624 · Garibaldi

Below: Looking south along the shoreline from the Neahkahnie Mountain Wayfinding Point on Highway 101, a few miles outside the old port of Nehalem.

The 101 continues south from Seaside, bypassing Tillamook Head, the 1,100-foot cliff scaled by Lewis and Clark in January 1806; Clark's journal describes how, at one point during their ascent of its almost sheer face, he and his companions "were obliged to Support and draw our selves up by bushes & roots." The road now approaches Cannon Beach—a pleasant, breezy place, especially favored by artists, many of whom exhibit and sell their work in its galleries and stores. It acquired its curious name when one of the cannons belonging to the U.S. navy schooner *Shark*, lost with all hands at the mouth of the Columbia River in 1846, was washed up on a nearby shore. Cannon Beach's Sunset Boulevard turnoff from 101 leads to a junction with its "beach loop" on Hemlock Street. Turn right here to explore the town center, or left to visit Tolovana Park, and to take a closer look at this area's most prominent offshore landmark: the 235-foot Haystack Rock.

After we rejoin 101 south of Tolovana, the road level rises considerably as it sweeps past Arcadia Beach, Hug Point and Arch Cape. The Oswald West

Above: This skilfully engineered section of 101 just south of Neahkahnie Mountain has been blasted out of the surrounding cliff face.

Left: A storefront on Hemlock Street in downtown Cannon Beach. The town is often described as "Oregon's Carmel."

State Park, dedicated to the Oregon governor who did so much to preserve this coastline (see pages 38–39), and the majestic, tree-covered peak of Neahkahnie Mountain—whose name is Amerindian for "Home of the Supreme Being"—are a few miles farther on. At the mountain's foot, near the northern edge of Nehalem Bay, lies Manzanita.

The Bay itself is now a popular destination for vacationers and fishermen, but until 101 arrived here in the 1930s, the region had poor road access, and the town of Nehalem itself was largely dependent on river and sea traffic. However, Wheeler, on the Bay's southern shore, had the advantage of being served by the Portland—Tillamook railroad that had opened in the 1900s. Despite the advent of the highway, its tracks remain in use, and during the summer, a "fun train" service carries tourists along the coast to Rockaway Beach, Garibaldi and Tillamook Bay.

45

STATE OF OREGON
1859
OREGON

| 0588 | Cannon Beach | 0608 | Nehalem | 0613 | Rockaway Beach | 0624 |
| Seaside | 0594 | Manzanita | 0610 | Wheeler | 0617 | Garibaldi |

Below: The view north along the shore from the verge of the 4 ½-mile 'Rough Road' south of Tillamook Bay. This route leads to the Cape Meares Scenic Viewpoint, the nearby Lighthouse (shown on pages 52-53) and the 'Octopus Tree.'

Beyond the "Garibaldi Beaches," as the shoreline south from Nehalem to Garibaldi was once called, we approach the outskirts of Tillamook, famously described as "the land of cheese, trees and ocean breeze;" its long history of dairy production is detailed on pages 26-27. The bay just to the northwest was explored in 1788 by Captains John Meares and Robert Gray, who discovered it within a month of each other. Meares named it "Quicksand Bay," but Gray, whose servant, Lopez, was killed by natives while his ship was at lying at anchor there, christened it "Murderers' Harbor." Bay and city have been known as Tillamook since the nineteenth century.

We enter Tillamook on 101, turn right onto 3rd Street, and head west out of town, eventually connecting with Bayocean Road. Here, we turn right again, following Bayocean as it skirts the southern edge of Tillamook Bay, before taking the signposted route to the Cape Meares State Scenic Viewpoint, an area rich in natural and historical interest. One of its best-known features is its lighthouse—built between 1888-90 and just 38 feet tall (the headland on which it stands is 217 feet above sea level). It can only be reached on foot, via a wooded pathway from the parking lot at the end of the road. The short walk offers superb views of the Cape's cliff face and sea caves; and the lighthouse itself, which was decommissioned in 1963, has been lovingly restored and incorporates a museum and gift shop.

*Above and left: The coastline at Cape Meares –
looking northeast, and southwest toward the next section
of the picturesque 'Three Capes Scenic Route.'*

*Right: The 'Octopus Tree', whose six huge limbs extend
some 30 feet from its main trunk. Its sheltered location
has helped it survive the onslaughts of wind and sea.*

Also close by the car park is the extraordinary
"Octopus Tree," known to local Indian tribes as the
"Council Tree." The base of this massive Sitka
spruce is over 50 feet in circumference, and its
"candelabra" branching is the result of constant
buffeting by sea winds. Its exact age is uncertain, but
some botanists believe it to be over 1,000 years old.

STATE OF OREGON 1859

OREGON

Bay City

0629

0633

Tillamook

Cape Meares

0642

0644

Oceanside

Netarts

0646

0652

Cape Lookout

Cape Kiwanda

0665

Above: The coast seen from Anderson's Viewpoint, north of Cape Lookout, showing Netarts Bay and Spit.

Below: Whale Cove, a little to the south of Depoe Bay. Gray whales can be spotted around here throughout the year, and the area is also a favored habitat for seals and other wildlife.

After returning to the coast road, we resume our journey along the "Three Capes Scenic Drive"—the 40-mile loop from Tillamook that brought us to Cape Meares, and now leads on towards two more southerly beauty spots, Cape Lookout and Cape Kiwanda. First, though, we pass the small settlements of Oceanside and Netarts. The former, originally known as Maxwell Point, began as a northern outgrowth of Netarts in the 1880s. Just off its shore are the Three Arch Rocks, "Shag," "Mid Rock," and "Storm Rock" (first spotted by Captain John Meares as he sailed north in 1778—he christened them "The Three Brothers"). They are home to thousands of seabirds, and have been a National Wildlife Refuge since 1907. Netarts, about two miles away, takes its name from the local Indian words "ne ta at"—"near the water;" across the bay on which it lies, the sandy, five mile-long finger of land known as Netarts Spit stretches to the north.

The spit is part of Cape Lookout State Park, whose entrance is south of the bay. It offers walking trails through lush forests to the Cape itself (a high headland jutting out to the west), and the area is also a favorite with paragliding enthusiasts and campers. Beyond it, we follow the Scenic Drive to Cape Kiwanda, a fine vista point that also boasts a "haystack"-shaped sea rock, before rejoining Highway 101 south of Pacific City.

The next sizeable place we encounter, Lincoln City, was created in 1965 from five smaller towns, and extends for several miles along the road. Its two most famous features are the Devil's Lake State Park (visible on the left of the highway), and the "D" River, whose course from the lake to the sea measures just 440 feet—earning it the official title of "shortest river in the world." The beach near its outflow, like much of Lincoln City's breezy coastline, is a popular location for kite and flag flying, but travelers looking for something a little more unusual may prefer to continue south to Depoe Bay, one of the best sites in this region for whale watching.

Left and below: The mouth of the tiny 'D' River – and the sign on Lincoln City's nearby 1st Street pointing out this easily missed landmark to passers-by. Originally known as the Devil's River, its name was changed after protests from religious leaders.

Below: A colorful kite flutters on the beach near the 'D' River. Kite-flying festivals, attracting thousands of visitors, take place in Lincoln City each Spring and Fall.

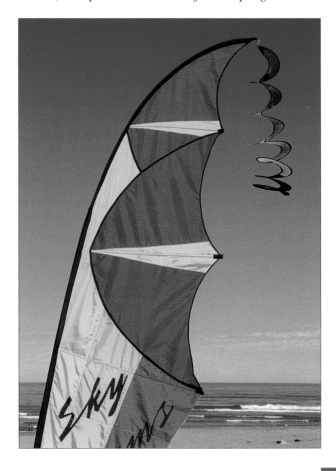

49

Below: Otter Rock's Flying Dutchman Winery. Its produce can be sampled and purchased here throughout the year.

Above: Ice cream, popcorn, candy, espresso and soda are available from this elegant 1930s Dodge truck operated by the Winery's owners.

Center (above and below): Looking north toward Cape Foulweather and Otter Crest (site of a successful hotel whose grounds can also be seen in the photo on the far right) from the owners' deck at the Flying Dutchman Winery.

The rocky promontory that Captain Cook named Cape Foulweather is about four miles south of Depoe Bay, on a section of the Central Oregon coastline that is notorious for high winds (often exceeding 100 mph) and heavy rain. Later mariners have described how gloomy and threatening it can seem when shrouded in fog—but on a clear day, it is an impressive sight from land or ocean, and an excellent place from which to look for sea lions, seals and other wildlife. Near here, Highway 101 climbs to 500 feet—its highest elevation in Oregon.

Just a mile from Cape Foulweather is the village of Otter Rock, and the turnoff taking us to the Devil's Punchbowl Viewing Point. The "punchbowl" is a basin-shaped crater below the cliffs that fills with sea-water as the tide comes in, and Otter Rock is also home to the Flying Dutchman Winery, opened in 2001 by Joanne Roberts and her husband Richard Cutler in elegant, century-old premises that previously served as a post office and pottery shop. The Cutlers produce their award-winning wines from grapes grown in the Willamette Valley, a little to the east; they offer regular tasting sessions, as well as non-alcoholic refreshments and gifts.

101 now makes its way along the coast towards Newport. A few miles north of the town stands the 93-foot Yaquina Head lighthouse (the state's tallest), which has been in use since 1893, and is the subject of some strange local legends. There have allegedly been ghostly apparitions on the nearby shore, the site of several shipwrecks; and the light itself is said to be haunted by a keeper who died while tending its lantern in the 1920s. More recently, it has featured in a successful mystery novel, Ron Lovell's *Murder at Yaquina Head* (2002). Visitors can gain admission to the lighthouse and its surrounding area for a small fee.

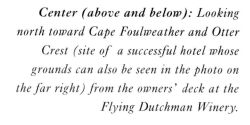

Above: Cape Foulweather and its surrounding coastline, photographed from Highway 101.

> " At day break the next Morning, the long looked for Coast of new Albion was seen extending from NE to SE distant 10 or 12 leagues… The land appeared to be of a moderate height, deversifed with hill and Vally and almost every where covered with wood… At the northern extreme, the land formed a point, which I called *Cape Foul Weather* from the very bad weather we soon after met with. "

Captain James Cook, Journal for March 7, 1778

Lighthouses

Above: Augustin-Jean Fresnel, inventor of the revolutionary lighthouse lens that bears his name.

Above and main photo: Oregon's Yaquina Head light.

Inset photos (clockwise): Santa Barbara lighthouse, California; Trinidad replica light and fog bell, California; Mark Abbott Memorial Light, Santa Cruz, California; Cape Blanco Light, Oregon; Cape Meares Light, Oregon.

Lighthouses are our constant companions on the Pacific Coast Highway—some, like the Yaquina Head light, easily accessible from the road, others perched on more remote rocks or headlands. Many date from the nineteenth century, and were built under perilously difficult conditions. The stone, bricks and metal required to make them often had to be brought in by ship, and construction was carried out by workers with little protection from wind or sea. Offshore lighthouse installation could be even more hazardous and expensive. In 1879, master mason John Trewares drowned at the site of Oregon's now abandoned Tillamook Rock light, which took three years to finish, and cost $123,000; the bill for the Destruction Island light near Ruby Beach in Washington State, completed in 1891, was a more modest, but still substantial $85,000.

One factor in the high price of lighthouses was the need for state-of-the-art lenses to focus the comparatively feeble output of the lanterns then in use. In 1852, the newly established U.S. Lighthouse Board directed that all the nation's lights should, where possible, be fitted with lenses designed by the French optical engineer Augustin-Jean Fresnel (1788-1827). These were more efficient than any previous devices, and the largest of them could produce a concentrated beam of light visible at least 20 miles out to sea. However, they had to be imported from Paris, delivered to each lighthouse, and assembled there; and the lenses for some West Coast lights had to be shipped around Cape Horn, adding further to the cost.

Fresnel lenses stayed in use until well into the twentieth century, though they have now mostly been replaced by more compact, lower-maintenance systems. But at a remarkable number of Pacific coast sites, this newer, automated technology still operates from the original Victorian lighthouse towers, whose role in safeguarding shipping and saving lives remains as crucial as ever.

Below: Thriving stores like this one have helped to make Newport's Bay Front the center of the city's long-established tourist trade.

Below: Near Newport's busy Bay Boulevard. Locally caught crab is a perennial favorite around Yaquina Bay.

Newport, our next stopping place in Central Oregon, is a former fishing village that was a fashionable seaside resort by the 1900s, and has subsequently become a significant regional center for commerce and tourism. Its main visitor attraction was once Nye Beach, a few blocks west of Highway 101 as it leads down towards Yaquina Bay, but today there is more to see on the town's Bay Front, with its colorful shops and busy marina. A nearby State Recreation Site contains the area's original lighthouse, first used in 1871, but later superseded by the more powerful light at Yaquina Head.

In the late nineteenth century, this region boasted extensive railroad and sea links, including a direct steamer service to San Francisco. However, these were eventually forced out of business by financial setbacks and navigational problems (Yaquina Bay, like Columbia River to the north, has a bar that can be dangerous to shipping), and since the 1930s, the bulk of Newport's passenger and freight traffic has been carried by 101.

The road heads over the Bay Bridge to the town's South Beach. Here, on Ferry Ship Road, is the Oregon Coast Aquarium, opened in 1992 and home to over 15,000 fish, mammals and other creatures. A few blocks away is another local institution: the Rogue Ale Brewery, founded by three ex-Nike executives in 1988, and now recognized as one of America's finest beer making companies.

Some 13 miles south of Newport, we reach Alsea Bay, named (like the river that flows into the Pacific there) for the Alsi Indian tribe who were its first settlers; on its southern shore is the old logging

Above: The Yaquina Bay Bridge, completed in 1936, was designed by Conde Balcom McCullough (1887–1946), Oregon's most distinguished bridge engineer.

Right and above right: *Two views of the Cape Perpetua Scenic Area – looking north along the shoreline to Yachats from beside Highway 101; and (a little farther along the road) the exquisite beach at Cape Cove.*

town of Waldport, a popular base for fishing and crabbing. Beyond it lies Yachats, and the northern edge of the 2,700-acre Cape Perpetua Scenic Area. The 700 foot-high Cape was christened by Captain James Cook, who first caught sight of it from the sea on St. Perpetua's Day (March 7), 1778; it is surrounded by dense forest and rocky beaches.

55

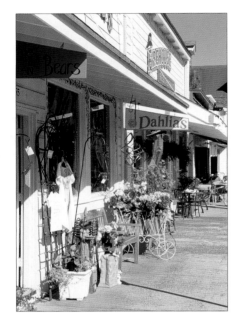

Above: Looking east down Bay Street in Florence's riverside Old Town area, with its elegant stores and restaurants.

Below: Small fishing craft moored at the Port of Siuslaw in Florence, just east of the roadbridge across the river.

Captain Cook is an inescapable presence on this coast; his name has even been attached to places he could never have seen from the deck of his ship, the *Resolution* —such as "Cook's Chasm," an undersea cave near Cape Perpetua that emits spectacular spouts of water at high tide. However, some 11 miles to the south, beyond the sandy expanse of Stonefield Beach, another famous navigator receives his just recognition. Heceta Head, which towers 1,000 feet above the sea here, was christened in honor of Bruno de Heceta (1744–1807), the Portuguese captain who sailed the northwestern Pacific three years before Cook; on its west side stands Oregon's most powerful lighthouse, the Heceta Head Light, completed in 1894.

The Head is only accessible to hikers; but the lighthouse, sited in the Devil's Elbow State Park, can be accessed by turning off 101 just before it reaches Cape Creek, and driving down to beach level via a tree-shaded road. This leads to a parking lot in easy walking distance of the assistant keeper's cottage (now offering bed-and-breakfast accommodation) and the light itself. Both buildings have recently been restored, and a modern 1.1 million-candlepower unit has replaced the 56-foot tower's original lamp. Returning to 101, we cross the Cape Creek Bridge and pass through a short tunnel; on its far side is a turnout providing superb views of the lighthouse and the huge colony of sea lions basking on the rocks below the highway. (More can be seen of these fascinating animals at the privately owned Sea Lion Caves, whose entrance is close by.)

After a few more miles of steep cliffs and dark, volcanic shorelines, the headlands recede and a long, uninterrupted beach stretches out before us. 101 moves a little inland as we approach the town of Florence, established on the Siuslaw River in the mid-nineteenth century; its Bay Street waterfront and nearby jetties are worth turning off the highway to explore. West of the Fishing Dock, 101 crosses the water, and continues towards the Oregon Dunes National Recreation Area.

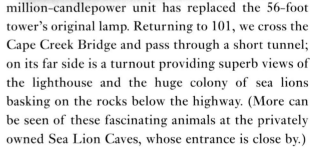

Left: BJ's, on Florence's Bay Street, offers no less than forty-eight flavors of home-made ice cream.
Below and far left: Heceta Head and its lighthouse, seen from Highway 101; the surrounding rocks are home to large seal populations.

Right: A 'trompe l'oeil' nightie, from Dahlia's in Florence.

STATE OF OREGON · **OREGON** · 1859

| Stonefield Beach | 0756 | Florence | 0786 | Reedsport | 0814 | Charleston |
| 0749 | Heceta Head | 0768 | Gardiner | 0789 | North Bend | 0823 |

Right: The cliffs and ocean at Sunset Bay State Park, an ideal location for camping, swimming and surfing. It acquired its name in the nineteenth century from Thomas Hirst, a resident in nearby Coos Bay.

The Oregon dunes, prosaically described by Captain Cook in 1778 as "white sand banks next to the Sea," are among the most extraordinary environments to be found anywhere on the Pacific coast. They stretch for 50 miles from south of Florence to Coos Bay, and there are many overlooks and other access points to them off 101. Walking the dunes can be arduous, but even a short climb onto the low sand hills west of the highway will provide a

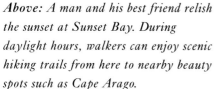

Above: A man and his best friend relish the sunset at Sunset Bay. During daylight hours, walkers can enjoy scenic hiking trails from here to nearby beauty spots such as Cape Arago.

Right: The famous Umpqua River light, in use for over a century, replaced an even earlier lighthouse, which was installed here in 1857, but swept away in a flood four years later.

fresh perspective on the surrounding landscape. To the left is the Siuslaw National Forest, which has bordered the highway for much of the last 60 miles. On the right lies a wide plateau of sand swept level by the wind; beyond it, a line of trees and other vegetation, followed by a rockier foreplain near the shore. The dunes are remarkably quiet; traffic seems to be muffled by the sand, although birdcalls and sounds from the sea can be heard clearly. The only noise capable of disrupting the peaceful atmosphere comes from the dune buggies that are allowed into parts of the Recreation Area!

Winchester Bay and the towns of Gardiner and Reedsport are approximately in the center of the dunes region. A few miles south of Reedsport, we turn west from 101 onto Salmon Harbor Drive, and then follow Lighthouse Way to the Umpqua River light—built, like its close twin at Heceta Head, in 1894. Unusually, both towers retain their original Fresnel lenses (see pages 52–53).

The road from the lighthouse loops back to 101, on which we continue south towards Coos Bay. After crossing the Bay, we turn onto Virginia Avenue (State Route 240) in North Bend. This soon becomes the Cape Arago Highway, and it takes us across the Bay's South Slough to Charleston, and along the coast to Sunset Bay—once a widely-used haven from rough seas for small boats, and now a popular and picturesque State Park.

The Oregon Dunes

The dunes are formed from sand that has been created, deposited and shaped by thousands of years of erosion, sea currents and westerly winds. They support a wide variety of plant and animal life, and were once an important hunting ground for Native American tribes. Later settlers used them (and similarly accessible shorelines) as makeshift roads before the advent of trains and paved highways, and sometimes grazed their cattle on them. During World War II, the dunes served as military target ranges, but were subsequently neglected—until, in 1972, pressure from ecologists led to the establishment of the 32,000-acre Oregon Dunes Recreation Area to safeguard their future. President Richard Nixon, who signed the legislation to create it, commented that "the dunes are as beautiful as they are unique—a mix of desolate whiteness with sparkling blue lakes and bright green foliage. Now this beauty may be preserved for all Americans for years to come."

Above: The Oregon Dunes Recreational Area – a vast, windswept nature reserve with an eerie charm all its own.

59

Shore Acres State Park

Below and bottom: The immaculate gardens of Shore Acres – a delightful surprise for most Pacific Coast Highway travelers.

Shore Acres, about a mile south of Sunset Beach, provides a dramatic contrast to the wild ocean scenery of the last few hundred miles. Beyond its gate lies an immaculately laid-out formal garden, boasting a fountain, hedged beds containing roses, rhododendrons, dahlias and other blooms, and—at its southern end—an Oriental-style pond with exotic plants and stone wading birds.

The story of the site's creation and survival is a remarkable one. In 1856, a wealthy lumberman and shipyard owner, Asa Simpson, established the town of Yarrow on Coos Bay. His son, Louis, took charge of it at the turn of the century, financing and supervising its expansion, renaming it North Bend,

and eventually becoming its mayor. As heir to the family business and fortune, Louis could afford to live luxuriously, and in 1906, he built an elegant summer residence for himself and his New York-born wife, Cassie, at Shore Acres. In the grounds of their new home, he planted flowers and shrubs from all over the world, many of them specially imported on his own ships; and house and gardens were soon growing steadily in size and sophistication.

In 1920, however, Cassie Simpson died, and the next year, the original Shore Acres mansion burned down. Louis replaced it (using timber from the cargo of a ship wrecked on the nearby coast), but his misfortunes were to continue: he sustained

severe financial losses during the Great Depression, and in 1936, parts of the estate, though not the house itself, were damaged in a second serious fire. In 1942, Shore Acres, now in poor shape, was acquired by the State of Oregon; the Simpson residence was demolished six years later, but the renovated gardens have become an enduringly popular visitor attraction. They are open every day, and thanks to the mild climate and the extensive range of species grown here, there are flowers in bloom throughout the year.

Above and left: Whatever the season, Shore Acres invariably has attractive flora on display. Different species of plants and flowers are meticulously labeled in their beds, and features like the fountain seen above (located at the center of the Botanical Garden) add to the Park's restful atmosphere.

Below: Looking north up Bandon's 2nd Street. The town, founded in 1853, owes much of its prosperity to cranberry growing, which began here in the late nineteenth century.

Above: A rope and mooring at the Sport Basin in Bandon's Old Town. The Basin, with its adjacent boardwalk, is especially convenient for the small boats used by Coquille River fishermen.

Louis Simpson's property originally extended well beyond Shore Acres, but in 1932, he deeded part of the southern section of it to the State of Oregon; the parcel of land included Simpson Reef, about a mile from his gardens. Visible from a roadside turnout, its rocks provide a perfect habitat for sea lions and other wildlife. A little farther on is the last of the three State Parks we encounter on this section of the coast. It surrounds Cape Arago, the 719-foot headland that has been a landmark to mariners ever since the English adventurer Sir Francis Drake saw it on his pioneering Pacific voyage in 1579.

Here, the highway deadends, and we double back towards Coos Bay. There are two alternative routes to 101 from this area. A right turn onto Seven Devils Road, 9 miles south of North Bend, leads to the South Slough National Estuarine Research Reserve, set up in 1974, and covering some 4,700 acres of marshland, mudflats and waterways. These can be explored on a variety of walking trails, and there is also an interpretive center (open Monday to Saturday) at the site. Seven Devils Road eventually rejoins 101 north of Bandon-By-The-Sea, but to reach the town more quickly, some travelers may prefer simply to return to North Bend and take the highway south from there.

Bandon has a nature reserve of its own on its northern outskirts, and the nearby Bullards Beach State Park contains the historic Coquille River lighthouse, dating from 1896. However, nothing remains of its original, mid-nineteenth century waterfront, which burned down in 1914. Bandon suffered a second, even more catastrophic fire in 1936, but subsequent rebuilding has preserved its original character, and the "Old Town" district is worth diverting from 101 to see—as is the beach loop road, accessible from 11th Street. This leads to Coquille Point, then south past Bandon Beach and a series of distinctive offshore rocks, the best-known of which is Face Rock—created, according to Native American legend, when an evil sea-spirit captured a beautiful young princess and turned her to stone.

> **"This country our generall named Albion, and that for two causes; the one in respect of the white bancks and cliffes, which lie toward the sea: the other, that it might have some affinity, even in name also, with our owne country, which was sometime so called."**
>
> *Sir Francis Drake (c.1540-1596)*, **The World Encompassed**

Above left: The 'Port Call' store on Bandon's 1st Street sells gifts with a nautical flavor, and is one of several Old Town businesses that can arrange boat charters for sea and river anglers.

Left and far left: The partially submerged rocks close to the beach at Coquille Point include the distinctively arched 'Elephant Rock', whose shape slightly resembles an elephant's body and trunk.

Below: On Highway 101 south of Port Orford – part of the Pacific Coast route designated a 'Scenic Byway' by the US Federal Highway Administration.

Bandon's Beach Loop Road reconnects with Highway 101 just south of the town's Face Rock Golf Course, and the main road continues through Langlois, about 16 miles away. Like Bandon (sometimes described as Oregon's "cranberry capital"), the little town is a center for fruit farming, and it is surrounded by roadside outlets selling homemade jam and similar produce.

101 has now moved further inland, but some 9 miles south of Langlois, we turn right onto Cape Blanco Road, and head back to the ocean. The Cape itself, Oregon's most westerly point, was sighted and named in January 1603 by the Spanish naval captain Martin de Aguilar, whose ship, the *Tres Reyes*, had set out from Acapulco on a voyage of exploration the previous year. (Sadly, Aguilar and several of his crew died before completing their journey.) Cape Blanco's lighthouse has been in continuous use since 1870, and during the summer months, there are regular tours of its 59-foot tower and outbuildings. There is also much to see in the surrounding State Park, which offers extensive walking and riding trails through more than 1,800 acres of beach and

riverside. On the Cape's northern edge is the historic Hughes ranch house, a lovingly preserved, two-story family dwelling, dating from 1898.

After making our way back to 101, we pass through Port Orford—the State's longest-established settlement, founded in 1851. It is especially famous for its locally grown, high-grade timber (the Hughes house at Cape Blanco was built from Port Orford cedar), and its recently improved harbor attracts both commercial and sports fishermen. South of the town is an exposed section of highway, bordered by steep cliffs and prone to high winds and slippery surfaces; it takes us beyond Humbug Mountain (a 1700-foot peak visible to the right of the road) and on towards the Rogue River and Gold Beach.

Above: The majestic sweep of beach at Cape Blanco State Park, looking north toward where the Sixes River enters the ocean.

Left and far left: The Cape Blanco site covers over 1,800 acres, and has almost enough "bleached, wind- and wave-swept driftwood" (to borrow a phrase from author Bill Harris) to rival the timber-strewn shores of Washington State, hundreds of miles to the north.

STATE OF OREGON

1859

OREGON

Cape Arago

0830

Shore Acres

0832

Charleston

0844

Bandon-By-The-Se

0829

Simpson Reef

0831

Sunset Bay

0835

North Bend

0869

Above: At the Pistol River Scenic Viewpoint, off Highway 101, looking · north to the bridge across the water. *Below:* Arch Rock stands just offshore a few miles south of Pistol River.

On its way to Ophir, 12 miles from Port Orford, 101 runs through a thickly wooded region. Forests to the left and rock faces to the right combine to shut out the sunlight, and at times the surrounding trees seem almost to form a canopy over the constantly twisting road. A little further south, the surroundings brighten as we move closer to the ocean—though the highway continues to dip and rise as it follows the contours of the shore.

Ophir takes its name from a Biblical city renowned for the quality of its gold, and this most precious of metals has had a considerable impact on the development of coastal Southern Oregon. Gold was discovered close to the mouth of Rogue River in 1853, and Wedderburn and Gold Beach have their origins in the mining camps that sprung up there.

The two villages' location made them staging posts for riverborne traffic, and in 1895, the first U.S. mail boat was dispatched upstream from Gold Beach—taking four days to complete its round trip to Agness, some 30 miles inland. The Rogue River mail service is still operational: high-speed hydro-jets are currently used for deliveries, as well as for tourist trips; these depart from the jetty on the north bank of the river near Wedderburn. A few yards away, 101 crosses the water and enters Gold Beach, whose attractions include a museum and a rival riverboat operation on Harbor Way.

About six miles from Rogue River, we pass Cape Sebastian, named in 1603 by Spanish naval commander Sebastian Vizcaino, leader of the expedition in which Martin de Aguilar (see pages

64–65) also participated. The highway now heads through a landscape of sand dunes near Pistol River, before reaching the more rugged coastline of the Samuel H. Boardman State Scenic Corridor—a protected area containing the 345-foot high Thomas Creek Bridge, and providing spectacular views of rock formations and beaches. Beyond it lie the port town of Brookings, and the border with California.

Left: These distinctively liveried Rogue River mail and passenger boats operate over 100 miles upstream.
Below: The mail boat jetty seen from the north bank of the Rogue River; near the Highway 101 road bridge.

California's Northern Coast

Much of the first stage of our journey through California is spent on Highway 101, which often seems to hurry us past the spectacular forests surrounding it—though there are opportunities to linger among the redwoods, and to turn off and explore the appropriately-named "Lost Coast" beyond Ferndale. At Leggett, 101 heads further inland, taking most of the traffic with it, and we can enjoy the more peaceful pace of Highway 1 as it leads south along the "Russian Coast" and towards San Francisco Bay.

Above: A window in the Officials' Quarters at Fort Ross, where Russian settlers lived and traded between 1812 and 1841. The fort, 21 miles north of Bodega Bay, is now a State Historic Park.

California's Northern Coast

Above: The California Western railroad (popularly known as the 'Skunk Train') runs from Fort Bragg inland to Willits (see pages 82–83).

"On the right side of the Indies there is an island called California… [The] island was the strongest in the world, with its steep cliffs and rock shores. [Its inhabitants' weapons] were of gold, as was the harness of the wild beasts they tamed to ride, for in the whole island there was no metal but gold." GARCIA ORDOÑEZ DE MONTALVO, *THE ADVENTURES OF ESPLANDIÁN*, 1510

This fanciful description, from a popular piece of early sixteenth-century Spanish fiction, contains the first known reference to "California." By the 1540s, the name was being applied to a real territory: a huge stretch of land (part of Spain's recently acquired viceroyalty, Nueva España) that included both the northwestern Mexican peninsula and the largely unknown region beyond it. Over the following two centuries, the Spanish assiduously explored and mapped the more accessible parts of

their vast possession; but they never succeeded in fully settling its northern reaches, which were soon attracting the attention of other Europeans and (eventually) Americans.

Spain believed that the strongest challenge to its sovereignty north of San Francisco came from Russia—but it is doubtful whether the Slavs who hunted the coastlines there, and later set up their own fortress near Bodega Bay (see pages 86–87), posed any genuine political threat. In fact, the Spanish finally lost control of California not through any foreign intervention, but as a result of Mexican independence in 1821; and Mexico itself was forced to

Below, left and right: Fort Bragg is also home to one of America's most celebrated beer makers, the North Coast Brewing Company.

Right: This totem-pole style decoration adorns a strikingly designed private garden in downtown Mendocino.

cede the province to the USA in 1848, after a military defeat. By now, California already boasted a sizeable population of American settlers, soon to be swelled by the "forty-niners" who arrived in the 1849 gold rush; in 1850, it became the thirty-first American state.

During this period, incomers from the Eastern United States and Europe were instrumental in establishing the lumber and fishing businesses that brought prosperity to much of the north Californian coast—and a few communities also took in migrants from more distant places. By the 1860s, the Mendocino area had over 500 Chinese residents (some of America's earliest Asiatic émigrés), who worked as loggers and miners, and assisted in the construction of Fort Bragg's "Skunk" Railroad (see pages 82–83). However, their numbers had fallen dramatically by the 1900s, partly as a result of the Chinese exclusion legislation passed in 1882. Many small towns in this region continued to rely on ships and horses for transportation until well into the twentieth century; and some sections of the Pacific Coast road, including a notorious stretch between Gualala and Jenner, were unpaved (and even blocked by farm gates!) for decades. Today, the only regular delays on Highway 1 are caused by maintenance and occasional stray cattle—though, with its dramatic bends and steep verges, it remains a slower, more challenging route to drive than the less picturesque Highway 101.

Below: A truckload of logs leaves a lumber yard on the edge of Lady Bird Johnson Grove (see next two pages).

Below The memorial to President F.D. Roosevelt in the Cathedral Grove at Muir Woods (see pages 90–91).

Above: The famous 'Chandelier Tree' in Leggett – one of several ancient, massive 'drive-thru' trees on this section of the road.

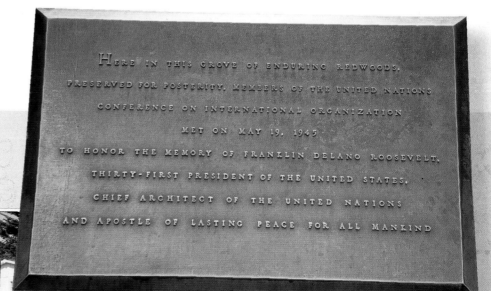

HERE IN THIS GROVE OF ENDURING REDWOODS, PRESERVED FOR POSTERITY, MEMBERS OF THE UNITED NATIONS CONFERENCE ON INTERNATIONAL ORGANIZATION MET ON MAY 19, 1945 TO HONOR THE MEMORY OF FRANKLIN DELANO ROOSEVELT, THIRTY-FIRST PRESIDENT OF THE UNITED STATES, CHIEF ARCHITECT OF THE UNITED NATIONS AND APOSTLE OF LASTING PEACE FOR ALL MANKIND

Left: An impressive display of topiary craft, seen beside Highway 1 in the seaside town of Manchester.

Above: The dedication of Lady Bird Johnson Grove. At the ceremony, Mrs. Johnson was praised for her "devoted service to the cause of preserving and enhancing America's natural beauty."

The first significant change in the landscape after crossing the Oregon-California border occurs a few miles beyond Crescent City, as the road is almost enclosed by a long stretch of trees, and motorists are instructed to switch on their headlights. We have reached the famous "Redwood Highway," a section of 101 that stretches from here to north of San Francisco—and over the next few hundred miles, there will be numerous opportunities to see the majestic trees around us at closer quarters.

Among the most spectacular of the roadside parks and groves in this region is the Trees of Mystery site near Klamath, some 16 miles south of

Above: The statues of Paul Bunyan and his ox Babe outside the Trees of Mystery at Klamath. Each weighs 30,000 lbs.

Crescent City. Massive statues of the mythical American backwoodsman Paul Bunyan, and his companion, a blue ox named Babe, stand in front of its entrance; but even these huge figures are dwarfed by the mighty coastal redwoods inside the gates,

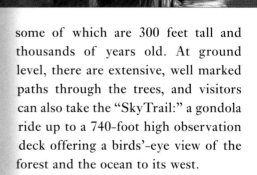

some of which are 300 feet tall and thousands of years old. At ground level, there are extensive, well marked paths through the trees, and visitors can also take the "SkyTrail:" a gondola ride up to a 740-foot high observation deck offering a birds'-eye view of the forest and the ocean to its west.

Back on the highway, we cross the Klamath river and continue south along 101. About 20 miles further on is a turnoff leading to another impressive tree-viewing area: Lady Bird Johnson Grove, named for the wife of former President Lyndon Johnson, and dedicated by President

> **"** Here sown by the Creator's hand
> In settled ranks the Redwoods stand;
> No other clime is honored so,
> No other lands their glory know. **"**
>
> *Joseph B. Strauss (1870–1938)*, **The Redwoods**

Above: The footbridge leading to the 1-mile walking trail though the trees of Lady Bird Johnson Grove.

Richard Nixon on August 27, 1969. The grove, with its ancient redwoods and Douglas-firs, is a fitting tribute to Mrs. Johnson, a committed conservationist and supporter of the state park system. At the dedication ceremony, she commented that the protection of America's natural environment was "indeed a bipartisan business because all of us have the same stake in this magnificent continent. All of us have the same love for it and… the same opportunity to work in our time to see that it stays as glorious."

Above: An elk gazes impassively at passing traffic on Highway 101 about a mile north of the turnoff for Lady Bird Johnson Grove. Some of his shyer companions are hiding in nearby trees.

Left: A pile of sawn tree-trunks awaiting collection near Orick. Logging operations are closely regulated throughout the redwood-growing region.

CALIFORNIA REPUBLIC

CALIFORNIA

| Smith River | 0980 | | Klamath | 1021 | | Trinidad | 1051 | | Arcata |
| 0967 | | Crescent City | | 0996 | Orick | | 1041 | McKinleyville | 1058 |

Below: William Carson, the Canadian-born entrepreneur who became the city of Eureka's principal employer and benefactor.

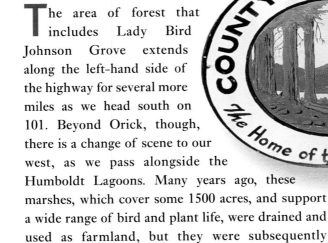

The area of forest that includes Lady Bird Johnson Grove extends along the left-hand side of the highway for several more miles as we head south on 101. Beyond Orick, though, there is a change of scene to our west, as we pass alongside the Humboldt Lagoons. Many years ago, these marshes, which cover some 1500 acres, and support a wide range of bird and plant life, were drained and used as farmland, but they were subsequently allowed to return to their natural state, and have been protected by State Park status since 1928.

We now approach the little port of Trinidad, a former Yurok Indian village named for the Portuguese navigator Bruno de Heceta (see pages 56–57), who sailed into harbor here on Trinity Sunday, 1775. A center for fishing and whaling, it was also a supply point for prospectors searching for gold north of Orick in the 1850s. The town's historic links with the ocean are commemorated by the replica lighthouse at the end of its Trinity Street (reached by taking the Main Street turnoff from 101 and then bearing left onto Trinity). This is an exact copy of the coal-oil powered light that stood on nearby Trinidad Head from 1871 to 1942. Next to it is the fog bell used at the same location until 1947; it has been electrified, and is rung at noon each day in remembrance of those lost at sea.

Back on 101, we continue down the coast towards Arcata, founded in 1850 (when it was known as Union); it is the home of Humboldt State

Below: Artist Duane Flatmo created this striking mural at Eureka's 4th and L Streets in 1990. It depicts Murray Field, one of the region's three airports.

University, the most westerly college campus in the United States. Arcata's closest neighbor is the largest city in this region, Eureka, established on the 10-mile long natural harbor of Humboldt Bay in 1850. Eureka made its fortune from logging, and a timber tycoon, William Carson (1833–1904), was responsible for creating its most outstanding and extraordinary building—the Carson Mansion on 2nd and M Streets, completed in 1886, and now an exclusive gentlemen's club.

Above: Eureka's opulent Carson Mansion, built for William Carson and his wife Sarah. Carson lived here until his death; the house was eventually sold by his family in 1950.

Breweries

This page: North Coast Brewing Company sign, Fort Bragg, CA; customers at Mike's Tavern, Raymond, WA, c.1910; a truck outside the Rogue Ale Brewery, Newport, OR.

The Pacific Coast Highway offers travelers with a taste for beer the opportunity to sample a succession of superb brews as they journey down the road. Every region has its own established favorites—from Redhook in Washington State and Rogue in Newport to classic Californian ales such as Anchor Steam and SLO Brewing Company's Gold-IPA—although it can sometimes be fun simply to take pot-luck, and ask the bartender which local brand he or she recommends!

Nearly all the companies responsible for these superlative ales started out as small, privately owned "microbreweries" making fewer than 15,000 barrels per year. A handful of them (including Anchor in San Francisco and Arcata's Humboldt brewery) can trace their heritage back to the

nineteenth century, but the majority date from the 1980s, when a combination of changing consumer tastes and more liberal legislation opened up the market for regionally-brewed beers, often sold from brewpubs owned by the producers.

The "micro" sector has grown remarkably over the following years — by 1993, there were over 12 times as many small breweries as in 1985, and numbers have continued to rise. As a result, some producers have increased their volume and gained national (and even international) distribution. However, their commitment to quality remains uncompromised; even in larger "craft breweries," beers are almost invariably produced by hand, under the supervision of brewmasters dedicated to preserving the distinctiveness and flavor of their brands. Larry Lesterud, Head Brewer at Humboldt, which has recently expanded its range of ales, and sells them throughout the Pacific northwest, commented in a

Above: The headquarters of the Humboldt Brewing Company, 10th and I Streets, Arcata, CA.
Left: The Lost Coast Brewery, 4th Street, Eureka, CA, founded by Wendy Pound and Barbara Groom in 1986.

recent interview that "The most significant trend I see in microbrewing is mainstreaming... Micros are now in most better restaurants and bars throughout the country, [and] the mass market is finally becoming aware that beer isn't just for guzzling in the frat house and after work in the shop."

After leaving Eureka, Highway 101 continues through Bayview and Fields Landing before reaching Fernbridge. Here, we exit onto Route 211, which leads southwest across a level landscape of pastures and grazing cattle, bringing us to Ferndale within about 5 miles.

In his informative illustrated guide to the Pacific Coast Highway, author Bill Harris described Ferndale as a place "where the clock seems to have stopped in about 1870." As we drive down Main Street on 211, we do indeed seem to have entered an architectural time warp; there are numerous authentic nineteenth-century structures, and many of the town's more recently-constructed frontages have been designed to match the prevailing style. Even the rest rooms have a suitably "period" blue-and-red finish! Notable buildings on Main include stores such as Ring's Pharmacy and the "Gazebo," both dating from the 1890s and still open to customers. At its junction with Washington, the street features a more modern curiosity—a scaled-down, pink and white "Victorian" created in 1995 by the owner of a local lumber company, Troy Land, and subsequently raffled to raise money for charity. The tiny house was won by a woman from Watsonville, near Santa Cruz, but its eventual re-sale to a Ferndale resident has allowed it to stay on display here.

A block away, at Brown and Berding, is Ferndale's most outstanding and best-known landmark, the "Gingerbread Mansion." Completed in 1899, it was originally the private residence of one of the town's physicians, Dr. Hogan Ring, but later served as a hospital, and as offices and apartments, before becoming a bed-and-breakfast inn. The mansion's interior is as striking as its façade and "English" gardens: Ken Torbert, the owner and proprietor since the early 1980s, has had its bedrooms, parlors and hallways restored to their former glory, decorated in period style, and furnished with antiques. The Inn enjoys the distinction of being awarded the American Automobile Association's coveted 'four-diamond' rating for seven years in succession.

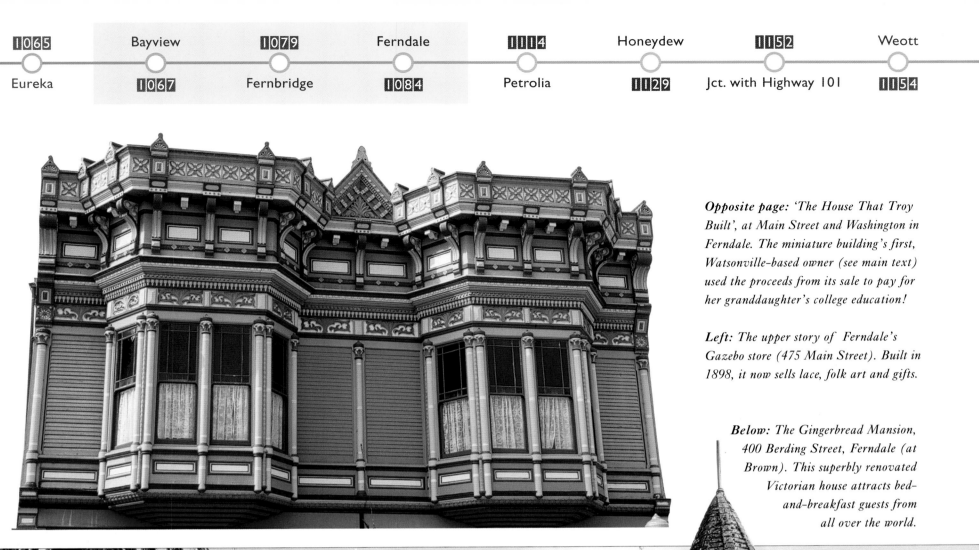

Opposite page: 'The House That Troy Built', at Main Street and Washington in Ferndale. The miniature building's first, Watsonville-based owner (see main text) used the proceeds from its sale to pay for her granddaughter's college education!

Left: The upper story of Ferndale's Gazebo store (475 Main Street). Built in 1898, it now sells lace, folk art and gifts.

Below: The Gingerbread Mansion, 400 Berding Street, Ferndale (at Brown). This superbly renovated Victorian house attracts bed-and-breakfast guests from all over the world.

CALIFORNIA REPUBLIC

CALIFORNIA

Bayview	1079		Ferndale	1114	Honeydew	1152	Weott
1067	Fernbridge		1084	Petrolia	1129	Jct. with Highway 101	1154

Coastal loop

Below: On the 'Avenue of the Giants' – this shady side road runs through the redwoods for over 30 miles.

The coastal highway beyond Ferndale is not for the faint-hearted. It is undoubtedly quicker and easier to return to 101 and continue south from there—but more intrepid travelers may be prepared to brave the gradients and bends of the road locals call "The Wildcat" in order to enjoy the sometimes desolate glory of its surroundings. Before embarking on this route, drivers should ensure they have enough gas; there are no services anywhere along its 68-mile length.

To take "The Wildcat," turn right onto Ocean from Ferndale's Main Street, then, almost immediately, left onto the road signposted "Petrolia." This rises steeply, then begins a long, twisting descent towards Cape Mendocino (the most westerly point in the continental United States), and runs almost level with its lonely, rocky shoreline. Further south, the forest closes in as we approach

embark on a seemingly endless climb—mostly in tree-covered gloom, though there are occasional glimpses of the woods' outer edge, bathed in brilliant sunlight—which finally brings us to a junction with 101 a couple of miles north of Weott.

The wide main highway will probably be a welcome relief after so many miles of back roads and hairpin turns. But should it become too monotonous, there is an alternative: the "Avenue of the Giants" runs close to 101 for the next few miles, providing a cool, dark passage between the mighty redwoods and through little settlements such as Myers Flat and Miranda, before

Petrolia, site of California's first, short-lived oil drilling operation in 1865. Beyond it, the highway crosses and re-crosses the Mattole River, weaving its way to Honeydew, some 15 miles away. We now

Above and left: The landscape on the long detour via Cape Mendocino has a stark, melancholy beauty, although visibility is often restricted by clouds and fog.

Right: Leggett's 'Chandelier Tree' has an arch at its base wide enough for most cars to pass through fairly easily – though drivers with larger vehicles (or protruding wing-mirrors) may need to take extra care!

ending south of Phillipsville. From here, we head for Leggett, where we take Highway 1 back to the coast—though not before checking out the town's most celebrated tourist attraction: its 315-foot "drive-thru" Chandelier Tree (believed by its owners to be some 2,400 years old), reached via a left turn just past the junction with 101.

CALIFORNIA REPUBLIC

CALIFORNIA

Weott

1158

1154   Myers Flat (exit)

Leggett

1208

1195   Rockport

Westport

1222

1239

Fort Bragg

Noyo

1241

Below: The elegantly mirrored interior of the North Coast Brewing Company Taproom and Grill, on Main Street in Fort Bragg, almost opposite the firm's main premises. Several of North Coast's award-winning premium beers (including Old Rasputin 'Russian Imperial' Stout, Acme IPA and Pale Ale, and Blue Star) are available on tap to customers.

For many travelers, Highway 1 is *the* Pacific Coast road, running south for more than 600 miles from Leggett to south of Los Angeles, and taking in some of the most celebrated and spectacular parts of our route through California. It starts by dropping some 2,000 feet to near sea level at Soldier Point, and then becomes Shoreline Highway, heading along the water's edge through Rockport and Westport before entering Fort Bragg.

The town, like its namesake in North Carolina, was christened in honor of General Braxton Bragg (1817–1876), a distinguished Mexican War commander who later fought on the Confederate side in the Civil War—though he never came here,

and the Californian Fort Bragg's military history lasted barely a decade. After the decommissioning of its garrison, set up in 1857 to watch over a nearby Mendocino Indian reservation, it developed into a center for timber sawing and shipping, and later acquired its own railroad (see panel opposite).

Fort Bragg sustained serious damage in the 1906 earthquake, but soon recovered its fortunes, becoming a major source of wood for the reconstruction of San Francisco, which had been devastated by the same disaster. Today, it is still a lumber town, but has diversified into fishing, tourism, and other enterprises, and is also home to one of the most successful of California's

Above qnd top: Two 'critturs' with special links to Fort Bragg… North Coast Brewing's Red Seal, symbol of the company's best-known beer; and California Western's railroad-riding (and stink-free!) skunk.

microbreweries—Mark Ruedrich's North Coast Brewing Company. This opened at 455 North Main in 1988, and has won a string of awards for ales and stouts like Red Seal, Acme, and Old No. 38. They can all be sampled at the firm's elegant Taproom and Grill, sited just across the street from its headquarters. Beyond here, Highway 1 continues south, crossing the mouth of the Noyo River that forms Port Bragg's harbor as it leaves town.

Above: This mural by Prete Giacinto, painted in 1993, adorns the wall of the California Western Depot in Fort Bragg.

The "Skunk Train"

Fort Bragg's railroad was the brainchild of Charles Russell Johnson (1859-1940), co-founder of the area's main lumber company. Launched, in 1885, as a freight line bringing logs to town for shipping, it began using steam locomotives and carrying passengers in 1904, and was named the California Western Railroad the following year. By 1911, the tracks reached as far as Willits, 40 miles to the east, and the next breakthrough came 13 years later, with the introduction of gas-powered engines whose distinctive smell gave the line its nickname—the "Skunk!" These locos, now converted to odor-free diesel operation, are still in service (along with a steam engine and a diesel-electric), ferrying tourists from the Skunk Train's striking downtown depot in Fort Bragg to Willits via Northspur. A one-way journey takes about 3 1/2 hours, and the railroad also offers various return trips and special excursions (see pages 188–189).

CALIFORNIA REPUBLIC

CALIFORNIA

| Weott | 1158 | Leggett | 1208 | Westport | 1239 | Noyo |
| 1154 | Myers Flat (exit) | 1195 | Rockport | 1222 | Fort Bragg | 1241 |

Above: Mendocino's Temple Kwan Tai, built on a 33 by 80 foot lot in the 1850s, is now a California State Landmark.

Above top: Masonic meetings still take place at the order's historic Mendocino Lodge, which also serves as a bank.

Mendocino, our next port of call, lies about 8 miles south of Fort Bragg; to reach its downtown area, turn off the Shoreline Highway at Little Lake Road, and drive a few blocks west. The strikingly picturesque surroundings here attract large numbers of tourists every summer, and have frequently been used as movie locations (notably for Elia Kazan's 1955 version of John Steinbeck's East of Eden, starring James Dean)—but there is a richly fascinating history to be discovered beneath the town's carefully groomed surface.

Mendocino's founders, who made their money from logging and sawmills, were responsible for elegant Victorian architecture such as the MacCallum House on Albion Street—a wedding gift in 1882 from a leading local businessman, William H. Kelley, to his daughter, Daisy MacCallum. Mrs. MacCallum had the five-bedroom mansion renovated and expanded following earthquake damage in 1906; it remained in her family until 1974, and is currently a luxurious inn and restaurant. Another celebrated period building, the Masonic Temple at Ukiah and Lansing, with its distinctive interior carvings and rooftop redwood statues, was completed in 1873; its features have been meticulously preserved by its present owners, the Savings Bank of Mendocino County.

It would be all too easy to overlook another significant, though much less outwardly impressive site: the Temple Kwan Tai (also known as the Mendocino Joss House), further down on Albion. Named for the Taoist god of war, it was constructed in about 1852 by the city's earliest Chinese population, who came here to work as loggers and miners, and is believed to be the oldest place of worship of its kind in Northern California. For many years, the temple was the property of the Hee family, the only remaining local residents directly descended from the original group of Asiatic settlers. Now run by a non-profitmaking trust, it has recently undergone major repairs, and was rededicated at a special ceremony in October 2001.

1244 Caspar

Mendocino
1247

1249 Little River

Albion
1253

1262 Elk

Manchester
1276

1280 Point Arena

Anchor Bay
1291

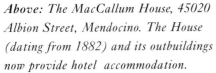

Above: The MacCallum House, 45020 Albion Street, Mendocino. The House (dating from 1882) and its outbuildings now provide hotel accommodation.

Right and left:Local resident Alan Sussex created these imaginative, colorful garden layouts on a vacant lot in downtown Mendocino which he purchased in 1979. More than 50 different species of plants and flowers are on display here.

Fort Ross State Park

Photos (clockwise from below): interior of Officials' Quarters; Kuskov House and chapel (chapel has two domes); chapel (with bell beside it) and cannon; view from southeast blockhouse showing Officials' Quarters and Rotchev House; Officials' Quarters and Rotchev House from a different perspective (with well in foreground).

Russian fur hunters had been active in the Aleutian Islands, off the Alaskan coast, since the 1740s. Within a few decades, they had settled on the mainland, but after exhausting stocks of sea otters and fur seals there, they were forced to head further south, and, by the early 1800s, were seeking their prey on northern Californian shores. In 1809, a temporary Russian hunting base was established on Bodega Bay (see next two pages). Its manager, Ivan Kuskov of the Russian American Fur Company, was instructed to find a suitable location for a more permanent colony; he selected a spot some miles to the north, and returned there in 1811 with a group of over 100 Russians and Alaskans to set up what became Fort Ross.

The fort, whose name was chosen for its similarity with the word Rossiya (Russia), was fully operational by the following year. It lies (just beside

Right: *The Fort Ross graveyard; this lies outside the stockade, which can be seen in the background of the photo, with the seashore to the left. Note the distinctively shaped Russian crosses marking the graves.*

Highway 1), some 60 miles down the coast from Mendocino—a remote area where there would have been little expectation of trouble from the Spanish authorities or local Indians. Nevertheless, it was protected with a 14-foot high stockade and two blockhouses, and designed, as a Russian official commented in 1830, to "appear... as being very strong and possibly even unconquerable." Within the stockade, which boasted a sallyport for direct access to the beach, was accommodation for senior employees (including houses for Kuskov and his successor, Alexander Rotchev), as well as stores and a chapel. Other workers slept outside the gates, where there were barns, dairies, and a threshing floor for crops grown in nearby fields.

Fort Ross was intended not only to be self-sufficient and profitable, but also to supply farm produce to the Russians' Alaskan headquarters. However, despite the best endeavors of its skilled and versatile employees, it turned out to be incapable of providing sufficient yields of fur or food, and in 1841, it was sold, for $30,000, to Swiss-born trader and explorer John Augustus Sutter. It has been a State Park since 1906.

CALIFORNIA REPUBLIC
CALIFORNIA

Anchor Bay — 1296 — The Sea Ranch — 1307 — Fort Ross — 1333 — Bodega Bay
1291 — Gualala — 1303 — Stewarts Point — 1322 — Jenner — 1343

Below: The Bear Valley Earthquake Trail – a short but fascinating round trip from the nearby Visitor Center.

T he thinly populated stretch of shore around Fort Ross offers little shelter from the elements, and is often swathed in fog, like so much of this coastline. Such conditions must have proved treacherous to the Russian and Alaskan boatmen, steering their kayaks through the surrounding rocks and reefs. However, they found easier hunting grounds along the banks of what came to be called the Russian River, although they knew it as "Slavianka" ("the pretty little Slav girl"). It flows into the sea near Jenner, about 11 miles beyond Fort Ross; after passing through the town, Highway 1 crosses the river close to Willow Creek, an area used by the colonists for crop growing.

The road now continues towards Bodega Bay, celebrated as the location for Alfred Hitchcock's *The Birds* (1963). Visitors may be surprised to find that the real-life bay does not have an especially

Above and right: On the Earthquake Trail, the San Andreas fault-line, which passes within a few yards of the pathway, is marked out by the blue sticks visible in the photographs. The archive pictures on the display board help to reveal the full extent of the devastation that occurred during the 1906 earthquake.

Above: Looking north across Bodega Bay from near the highway. The town shares its name with the tiny village of Bodega, a few miles farther inland.

large wildfowl population; the vast flocks that so terrified moviegoers were created using a combination of specially brought-in birds and trick cinematography. A few miles to the south, a narrow channel of water displaces the open sea to our right as we enter Tomales Bay; across it lies Tomales Point and the Point Reyes peninsula.

This National Seashore is accessible via the Bear Valley Visitor Center, off Shoreline Boulevard in Olema, a little further on. From here, roads lead to the historic Point Reyes Lighthouse, and to Drake's Bay—one of the many possible places where the English mariner Sir Francis Drake (see pages 62–63) may have come ashore in the sixteenth century. The Center is also the starting point for hiking trips to more remote beaches and headlands, but the most rewarding short tour it offers is the Earthquake Trail—a half-mile pathway leading along the San Andreas fault-line, and showing where the ground shifted during the devastating earthquake that struck this region in 1906.

"Dust, Ashes and Desolation"

The words above were used by a journalist for Scribner's Magazine *to describe the scene in San Francisco several months after the 1906 earthquake had torn the city apart. The first tremor occurred at 5.12 am on Wednesday, April 18 that year; it was followed, almost immediately, by a main shock lasting about a minute, whose epicenter was close to Olema. The Bay Area sustained the worst damage (compounded by a subsequent series of fires in San Francisco that wiped out entire neighborhoods), but the earthquake also inflicted varying degrees of destruction from southern Oregon to central California. According to official figures, approximately 3,000 people died in the catastrophe; property worth over $500 million was lost.*

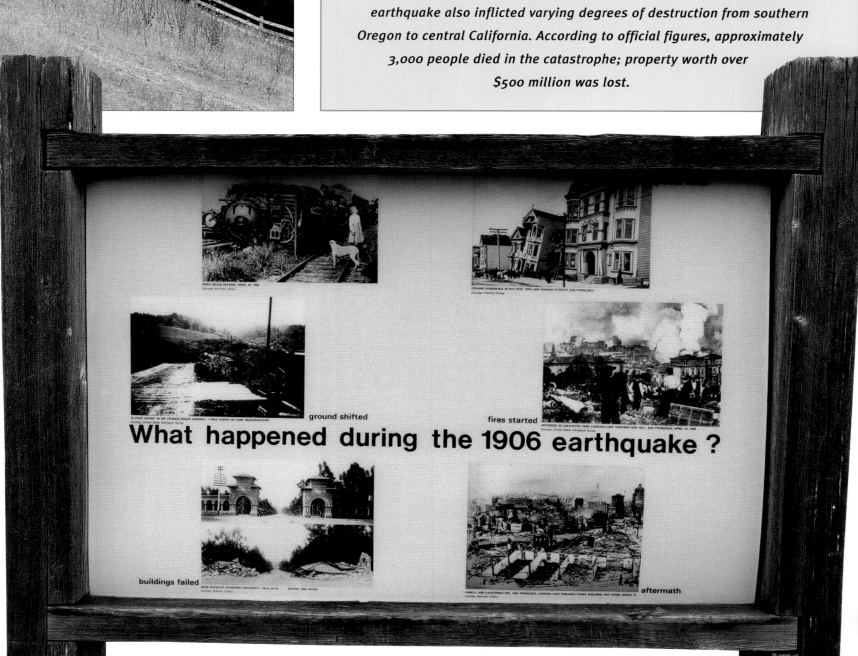

ground shifted

fires started

What happened during the 1906 earthquake?

buildings failed

aftermath

CALIFORNIA REPUBLIC

CALIFORNIA

Anchor Bay | 1296 | The Sea Ranch | 1307 | Fort Ross | 1333 | Bodega Bay
1291 | Gualala | 1303 | Stewarts Point | 1322 | Jenner | 1343

Below right and below: Looking south down Highway 1 between Stinson Beach and Muir Beach; and the mighty forest of Muir Woods, visited by over a million visitors every year.

As we approach San Francisco, roads become busier, and billboards, traffic lights, and other elements of city life start to encroach on the peaceful isolation we have enjoyed for so many miles. However, during the first part of our journey from Olema, nature still dominates, and there is no shortage of striking scenery—from the majesty of Mount Tamalpais (the Bay Area's highest peak, reached via the Panoramic Highway turnoff at Stinson Beach), to the golden sand and craggy headlands visible closer to the road. Muir Beach, about 5 miles south of Stinson, also contains some curious military leftovers—the derelict "base-end" gun-sighting stations built there (and at other locations along this coast) in 1940, but decommissioned after World War II.

Near the highwayside overlook to Muir Beach is an exit onto the road for Muir Woods—the only ancient redwood forest in this region, covering over 500 acres and containing trees that are thousands of years old. A philanthropist and future U.S. Congressman, William Kent, bought the woods for the nation in 1905. They were declared a National Monument by President Theodore Roosevelt three years later, and named (at Kent's suggestion) for the Scottish-born conservationist John Muir, whose lifelong efforts to preserve America's wild places played a major part in the setting up of the National Parks Service in 1918. Walking in Muir Woods is an

unforgettable experience, and there are numerous self-guiding trails and paths through its towering trees. Of especial interest is the Cathedral Grove (just over half a mile from the Visitor Center); in May 1945, a plaque in memory of President

Franklin D. Roosevelt was placed here by delegates to the San Francisco conference held prior to the signing of the United Nations Charter.

We now return to Highway 1 and continue towards San Francisco Bay. The road merges with Highway 101 for the final few miles prior to reaching the Golden Gate Bridge; just before crossing it, take the Alexander Avenue exit, and drive a little way along the Marin Headlands for a breathtaking view across to the far shore.

Above: The Golden Gate Bridge –
"the bridge at the end of the continent"
– seen from the Marin Headlands on
the north side of San Francisco Bay.

San Francisco to Monterey

The influence of Spain on the regions we have encountered so far has been largely a matter of place names and historical anecdotes. However, San Francisco gives us our first real taste of the Spanish Californian architecture and traditions which will be all-pervasive for the rest of this journey. South of "The City," we head down the coast towards the old mission settlement of Santa Cruz, before arriving at Monterey—now primarily a tourist town, but once the center of government and trade for the entire state.

Above: Workers' shacks on what was originally Ocean View Avenue in Monterey. The road was subsequently renamed for its celebrated fictional counterpart: John Steinbeck's 'Cannery Row.'

CALIFORNIA REPUBLIC
CALIFORNIA

Golden Gate
Bridge

San Francisco
(Presidio)

1431

Pacifica

1448

Half Moon Bay

1491

1419
Daly City

1439

Moss Beach

1453

Davenport

San Francisco to Monterey

Above: *Sunflowers, as well as a wide range of vegetable produce, are grown and sold beside Highway 101 on the Peninsula south of San Francisco.*

A visitor's first glimpse of San Francisco is capable of inspiring wonder and eloquence in equal measure—and the description by Scotsman Robert Louis Stevenson in *Across the Plains* (1879) of his arrival there by ferry at dawn is one of the finest ever written, conveying the smooth perfection of the sea ("not a ripple, scarce a stain, upon its blue expanse"), and the magical moment when "the city... and the bay of gold and corn, were lit from end to end with summer daylight."

The Spanish explorers who had discovered the same region just over a century earlier were similarly unable to conceal their excitement at what they saw. Their official diarist, Father Juan Crespi, though lacking Stevenson's literary gifts, managed to outdo him in hyperbole when he recorded their find of "a large and very fine harbor, such that not only all the navy of our most Catholic Majesty but those of all Europe could take shelter in it." Crespi's masters shared his opinion of the Bay's potential; within a few years, its shore had been fortified and settled, and by the early 1800s, it was second only to Monterey in strategic and commercial significance.

San Francisco overtook the then Californian capital as a center for shipping and trade after the Gold Rush of 1849, and despite subsequent fluctuations in the markets, and the ever-present threat of fire and earthquake, the city retained much of its boomtown prosperity for the rest of the century. It also became an axis for overland transportation—both long-distance (via the Union Pacific/Southern Pacific transcontinental railroad, launched in 1869), and more local. According to historian Rick Hamman, a daily stagecoach between San Francisco and Santa Cruz (with connections to Monterey) was in operation by the

Below: *A car cautiously descends San Francisco's "Crookedest Street" – the section of Lombard Street between Hyde and Leavenworth on the city's elegant Russian Hill, boasting no less than eight hairpin bends.*

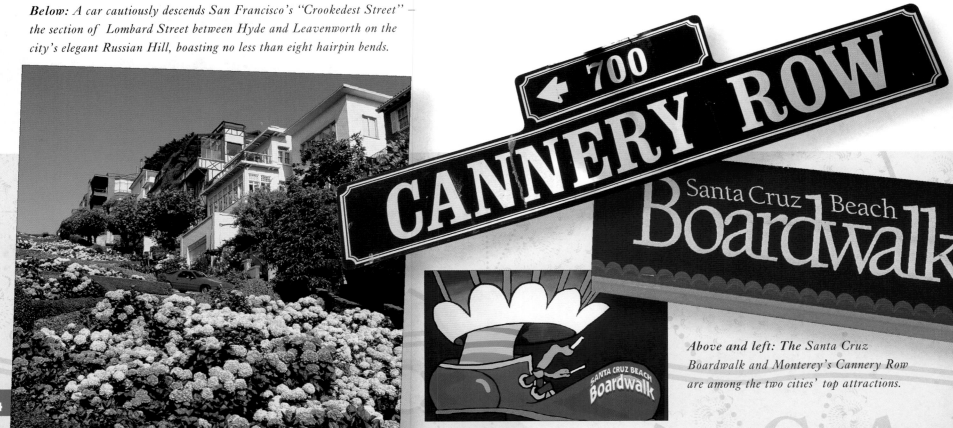

Above and left: *The Santa Cruz Boardwalk and Monterey's Cannery Row are among the two cities' top attractions.*

early 1860s, and this was later augmented by a freight and passenger railroad service to Watsonville.

In 1905, work began on the ill-fated "Ocean Shore" line, intended to reach from San Francisco to Santa Cruz; its tracks were never completed, and in the mid-1920s, coastal residents began lobbying for the disused rail bed to be converted into a highway. At first, the idea was opposed by the authorities in San Francisco, but by the end of the decade, they had relented, and what became the Pacific Coast road in the region was soon under construction. Eventually extended to Monterey, it provided a much-needed thoroughfare for the seaside towns inadequately served by Highway 101, and it remains a gloriously scenic alternative to the main north-south routes. It is also fairly easy and restful to drive—except, perhaps, on the sections that have been "upgraded" to freeway status!

Right: The Golden Gate Bridge seen from the San Francisco shore.

Right: Farmer John's Pumpkins, Half Moon Bay.

Below: The once rough Cannery Row is now well groomed for visitors.

Above: Fisherman's Wharf in Monterey.

CALIFORNIA REPUBLIC

CALIFORNIA

Golden Gate
Bridge

San Francisco
(Presidio)

1419

1431

Daly City

Pacifica

1439

1448

Moss Beach

Half Moon Bay

1453

1491

Davenport

Below: San Francisco's Lincoln Park Golf Course lies beside the ocean just southwest of the Presidio. Dating from 1908, it is home to the annual San Francisco City Championship – founded in 1917, and the oldest municipal golf tournament in the USA.

The path taken by the Pacific Coast road through San Francisco is a rapid and straightforward one. Almost immediately south of the Golden Gate Bridge, designed in the 1930s by civil engineer and sometime poet Joseph B. Strauss (see pages 72–73 for an example of his verse), Highway 1 splits away from 101, entering a tunnel under the city's original military stronghold, the Presidio, crossing Golden Gate Park, and heading south via the Sunset and Parkside districts. However, this route gives only a cursory glimpse of San Francisco's glories—and the following pages offer a few sightseeing suggestions for travelers who prefer to linger here a little.

First-time visitors could do worse than to continue into town on Highway 101, and look for a hotel on Lombard Street in the Marina neighborhood. Lombard, although not the most consistently picturesque of San Francisco thoroughfares, is an excellent base from which to explore the city's famous waterfront. Close by lie Fort Mason, the stores and cafés of Ghirardelli Square, and the gaudy combination of genuine local color and tourist attractions around Fisherman's Wharf. From here, a succession of numbered piers extends east around the edge of the Bay. Interesting sights include the *S.S. Jeremiah O'Brien*, one of the

"Liberty Ships" built at Henry Kaiser's yards just across the water in Oakland during World War II; she is moored at Pier 45 (Pier 32 in winter), with the *Pampanito*, a submarine from the same period, alongside. Also close by are departure points for

Right: S.S. Jeremiah O'Brien, built in just 56 days in 1943, served the Allied forces in both the Atlantic and Pacific during World War II.

Below: The Dutch Windmill on the northwestern edge of Golden Gate Park, seen from Bernice Rodgers Way.

ferries to the East Bay and excursions to Alcatraz Island—as well as a colony of alternately boisterous and sleepy sea lions alongside Pier 39.

For more peaceful surroundings, take the "Scenic Drive" along the city's western shoreline. The Great Highway runs parallel to the Pacific and past Golden Gate Park, one of America's oldest and largest city parks, whose 1,000-plus acres contain gardens, lakes, museums, and many other delights.

The Origins of San Francisco

In November 1769, San Francisco Bay was discovered and named, in honor of St. Francis of Assisi, by a party of Spaniards attached to the "Sacred Expedition" charged with setting up missions and military outposts in California (see next two pages). This advance group traveled overland to the Bay; the first Spanish ship arrived there in 1775, and its commander, Juan Miguél de Ayala, was responsible for choosing sites for the Presidio and Mission established in the area by Lieutenant Colonel Juan Bautista de Anza and Fr. Francisco Palóu the following year. However, modern San Francisco originated from a harbor settlement at a slightly different location: Yerba Buena (Spanish for "good herb"), founded in the 1830s on a stretch of San Francisco Bay well to the east of the Presidio.

The Missions

Right: Mission San Luis Rey de Francia, 4050 Mission Avenue, c.4 miles east of Oceanside. The Mission was founded in 1798; the church seen here was completed in about 1815.

Above: Mission Dolores Basilica, Dolores & 16th Streets, San Francisco. This building, largely dating from 1926, stands just to the right of the city's original Mission San Francisco de Asís.

The creation of missions in California was Spain's response to the perceived threat to its empire from Russia (see pages 86–87). The scheme was the brainchild of José de Gálvez, who had been dispatched from Madrid as visitador-general of Nueva España in 1765. His "Sacred Expedition" was launched from La Paz and Loreto four years later; it comprised two overland parties of Franciscan priests, soldiers and servants, as well as three ships, one of which was subsequently lost. In overall charge were a military man, Don Gaspár de Portolá, and a missionary, Father Junípero Serra: their orders were to establish a strong Spanish presence in the little-known territory to the north, and to convert its native population to Catholicism.

Portolá and Serra made their way from Loreto to San Diego; here, Serra supervised the building of a simple wooden chapel, and dedicated it on July 16, 1769. The following year, he came to Monterey to consecrate a second place of worship; initially, it shared a site with the presidio fortified by Portolá, but was moved to Carmel in 1771. These early settlements, which were soon expanded and strengthened, were gradually augmented by other missions and presidios—though progress was hindered by insufficient supplies and a shortage of troops to guard the vulnerable outposts.

Serra, as "Father-President" of the California missions, personally founded seven more of them before his death in 1784. Within fourteen years, a chain of twenty-one religious houses, stretching from San Diego to Sonoma, north of San Francisco, had been completed. They served as staging posts along the once hazardous route to and from Mexico; each mission was no more than a day's journey from its closest neighbor, and the trail that linked them together became known as *El Camino Reál* (The King's Highway). Even after Spain and Mexico lost control over California, this road retained its importance; north-south stagecoaches adopted it in the nineteenth century, and today, Highway 101 still follows its path in many places.

EL CAMINO REAL

THIS PLAQUE IS PLACED ON THE 250TH ANNIVERSARY OF THE BIRTH OF CALIFORNIA'S APOSTLE, PADRE JUNÍPERO SERRA, O.F.M. TO MARK THE NORTHERN TERMINUS OF EL CAMINO REAL AS PADRE SERRA KNEW IT AND HELPED TO BLAZE IT.

1713 · NOVEMBER 24 - 1963

CALIFORNIA REGISTERED HISTORICAL LANDMARK NO. 784

PLAQUE PLACED BY THE CALIFORNIA STATE PARK COMMISSION IN COOPERATION WITH THE COMMITTEE FOR EL CAMINO REAL.
NOVEMBER 21, 1963

Left: A commemorative sign celebrating Fr. Serra's achievements, erected adjacent to the Mission San Francisco de Asís in 1963.

Below: The beautiful courtyard and ornamental fountain of the Mission San Carlos Borromeo de Carmelo. Fr. Serra is buried in the Mission's chapel.

CALIFORNIA

Golden Gate Bridge | San Francisco (Presidio) | **1419** | **1431** | Daly City | Pacifica | **1439** | **1448** | Moss Beach | Half Moon Bay | **1453** | **1491** | Davenport

Below: As San Francisco's oldest surviving building, the Mission Dolores is a 'must-see' for visitors.

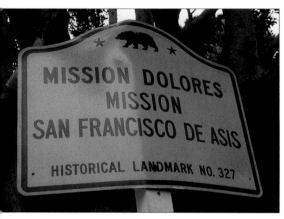

The San Francisco de Asís Mission is at 16th and Dolores, south of Market Street; the easiest way to get to it from the Marina district is to take Van Ness Avenue south from Lombard to its junction with 16th. The Mission chapel, located to the left of a larger, twentieth-century basilica, was completed in 1791, and was once part of a now-vanished quadrangle made up of cloisters, living quarters and storerooms. It replaced the original, mud-and-wood church built just east of here in 1776, and is popularly known as "Mission Dolores," after the name ("Nuesta Señora de los Dolores"—"Our Lady of Sorrows") given to a nearby creek and lake by early Spanish settlers. The chapel is still in regular use for worship, and is also open to visitors.

From the corner of Dolores, we head east for a few blocks, and then turn south onto Mission Street, which soon begins a slow climb past a succession of garish storefronts and billboards, most of them in Spanish—the first language of many residents in this area. After several miles' steady ascent, we detour onto San Jose Avenue (due to a local one-way system), cross the San Francisco County line, and rejoin Mission, now shown on signs and maps as Route 82, on the edge of Daly City.

Above: Remarkably, the old Mission Dolores survived the 1906 San Francisco earthquake undamaged – unlike the modern church next door.

Founded in 1911 on land owned by former dairy farmer John Daly (1840–1923), this suburb has been the butt of many disparaging comments over the years. It was most famously lampooned in the song *Little Boxes*, composed by Malvina Reynolds in 1962, which poked fun at the uniformity of its inhabitants' houses (and their lives). Today, such criticism seems a little excessive: Daly City's streets are pleasant, colorful, and scarcely less varied than those in some surrounding districts, while its hilltop air is clean and bracing. Beyond and below the town lies the San Francisco Peninsula; we reach it by taking I-280 and Highway 1 towards Pacifica.

Far right and far right above: Looking along San Jose Avenue, near Flournoy Street in Daly City. The homes on this agreeable residential street have none of the drab uniformity that songwriter Malvina Reynolds once observed here.

Above: On the corner of Flournoy and San Jose – 'a pink one and a blue one' that don't look quite the same!

> **Little boxes on the hillside,**
> **Little boxes made of ticky tacky,**
> **Little boxes on the hillside,**
> **Little boxes all the same,**
> **There's a green one and a pink one**
> **And a blue one and a yellow one**
> **And they're all made out of ticky tacky**
> **And they all look just the same.**

Malvina Reynolds (1900–1978), Little Boxes

101

| | | San Francisco (Presidio) | | 1431 | | Pacifica | 1448 | Half Moon Bay | | 1491 |
CALIFORNIA | Golden Gate Bridge | | 1419 | Daly City | | 1439 | Moss Beach | 1453 | Davenport |

CALIFORNIA

Below: *San Gregorio State Beach, near the junction of Highway 1 and La Honda Road (Highway 84), south of Half Moon Bay.*

Below: *Farmer John's Pumpkin Farm, 800 North Cabrillo Highway, Half Moon Bay. This award-winning roadside farm grows an extensive range of produce, and welcomes visitors.*

Highway 1—named the Cabrillo Highway throughout this region, in honor of Juan Rodríguez Cabrillo, the sixteenth-century navigator who discovered San Diego Bay—now sweeps down towards the sea and past Pacifica. Established in 1957, the town is regarded as California's "Fog Capital;" however, the weather here is clearest in late Summer, and every September since 1986, Pacifica has played host to a "Pacific Coast Fog Fest," described as "a celebration of sun, sand, and surf."

In the 1920s and 30s, the surrounding shoreline was often associated with less innocent activities. A few miles beyond Pacifica lies Moss Beach, site of "Frank's Place" (now the Moss Beach Distillery), notorious during the Prohibition Era as a hangout for illicit drinkers, and as a delivery point for black-market alcohol bound for San Francisco. Its owner, Frank Torres, had friends and protectors in high places, and his

lucrative speakeasy was allowed to operate without police interference. After Prohibition, "Frank's Place" became a legitimate, highly rated restaurant, and it still offers its customers fine food and drink, as well as a spectacular ocean view from its dining room and patio. To reach the Distillery, turn right off Highway 1 at Cypress Avenue in Moss Beach.

As we approach Half Moon Bay, pumpkin fields, and stalls offering a range of other fresh vegetables and fruit, begin to appear by the roadside. On Higgins Purissima Road, just south of the town center, is something more unexpected and even incongruous: a New England-style farmhouse, built in 1853 by a settler from Ohio, James Johnston, and now the oldest surviving residential building in this area. The house, which is currently undergoing

Above: Grey Whale Cove Beach lies a few miles to the north of Half Moon Bay.

Right and above right: *The James Johnston House, outside Half Moon Bay; and pumpkin fields near Denniston Creek Road, off Hwy. 1 near Moss Beach.*

restoration, is not open to the public, but its striking exterior is worth taking a short detour to examine more closely.

Further south, we pass San Gregorio and Pescadero Beaches (where the wind can sometimes whip up dense clouds of sand and dust across the highway), and the 115-foot tall Victorian lighthouse at Pigeon Point, before leaving San Mateo County and heading for Santa Cruz.

CALIFORNIA REPUBLIC

CALIFORNIA

Golden Gate
Bridge

San Francisco
(Presidio)

|1419|

Daly City

|1431|

Pacifica

|1439|

Moss Beach

|1448|

Half Moon Bay

|1453|

|1491|

Davenport

Below: The perennially attractive Santa Cruz Boardwalk has been providing beachside fun to locals and tourists for the past hundred years.

Below: Breakfast by the Bay...this eaterie offers a fine vantage point from which to survey the nearby waterfront.

The Santa Cruz region was given its name by Don Gaspár de Portolá (see pages 98–99), who came here in 1769, though it was not settled by Europeans until 1791, when Fermín Francisco de Lasuén, Junípero Serra's successor as Father-President of the California Missions, established the "Misión la exaltación de la Santa Cruz" on the banks of the San Lorenzo river.

The town that grew up nearby was initially a logging, farming and fishing community, but later became famous as one of the West Coast's first seaside resorts. Well-heeled guests were attracted to upmarket hotels such as the St. George, opened by millionaire businessman Anson P. Hotaling in 1895, and acclaimed by William Randolph Hearst as "the finest [place to stay] between San Francisco and Monterey." However, the greatest boost to the local

tourist industry came from entrepreneur Fred Swanton, creator of the famous, still-popular Beach Boardwalk and funfair at the start of the twentieth century (see below), and subsequently the city's mayor. Swanton also succeeded in persuading several early moviemakers to shoot their pictures in Santa Cruz—and more recently, director Alfred Hitchcock was said to have modeled the infamous Bates Motel in *Psycho* (1960) on a now-defunct downtown inn.

Santa Cruz's waterfront is reached from Highway 1 by taking a right onto Bay Street, continuing southeast to the junction with West Cliff, and then turning left and heading downhill to Beach Street and the Beach Boardwalk entrance. The heart of Fred Swanton's 1907 development remains intact (the original Boardwalk, dating from 1904, was destroyed

Above and above right: The Beach Street entrances to two major Santa Cruz Boardwalk attractions – Neptune's Kingdom and the Casino Arcade.
Right and above centre: Fresh seafood is available from stalls and restaurants on the Municipal Wharf, which also hosts an annual Clam Chowder Festival.

by fire two years later), although most of the funfair rides and arcade games on offer are modern ones. The area is colorful and exciting, though undeniably noisy when in full swing, and visitors seeking a quiet stroll and a breath of refreshing sea air may find the adjacent Wharf more to their taste. It is another longstanding institution, built in 1914 and boasting an excellent view across Monterey Bay, as well as a selection of shops and eateries.

CALIFORNIA

Golden Gate Bridge

San Francisco (Presidio)

1419

Daly City

1431

Pacifica

1439

Moss Beach

1448

Half Moon Bay

1453

1491

Davenport

Before leaving Santa Cruz's bayfront, go back up onto West Cliff Drive, and follow the road around to Lighthouse Field State Beach. The area of ocean below us is especially popular with surfers, and the lighthouse standing here, a working replica of one erected in 1869, serves both as a museum of the sport, and as a memorial to Mark Abbott, a young surfer who was killed nearby in 1965 (see panel). An inscription, placed beside its door by Mark's parents, dedicates the building "to all youth whose ideals are the beacons for the future."

Above, top and right: A plaque outside the Holy Cross Catholic Church at 126 High Street, Santa Cruz, marks the original location of the Mission Santa Cruz chapel; the other two photographs, taken at the Mission State Historic Park on School Street, show the exterior of a building used to accommodate neophytes, and a carreta *(cart) standing nearby.*

We now return to the West Cliff/Bay Street junction, head northwest on Bay, and then turn right (east) onto Mission Street, which leads towards the Mission Santa Cruz. The State Historic

Park containing its only surviving section, an adobe structure built in about 1822 to house Native American "neophytes" (converts), is on School Street, near Mission Plaza. The church on the site was destroyed by an earthquake in 1857—the last in a string of misfortunes that led to the settlement being dubbed the "bad luck mission." Its first, riverside location proved too damp, and was abandoned within a year of its foundation in 1791. Physical conditions were better at its present, hilltop position, but there were persistent problems with poor crop yields and hostile neighbors; and in 1812, one of the resident priests, Father Quintana, was murdered by a group of neophytes. The Mission was secularized by the Mexican government in

Chuck Abbott's Lighthouse

Chuck Abbott, a wealthy businessman and photographer, settled in Santa Cruz in 1963. Following the death of his 18-year old son, Mark, in a surfing accident two years later, Mr. Abbott and his wife, Esther Henderson, sponsored the construction of a new lighthouse for the city's harbor, dedicated to Mark's memory. (The original Santa Cruz light had been decommissioned in 1941 and removed in 1948). As he later explained to local historians Sharlene and Ted Nelson, "Our family had always loved lighthouses, so we decided it was the best thing to do." The building was completed in 1967; it is made from brick, and contains a lantern transplanted from a lighthouse once installed on San Francisco's East Bay. Mark Abbott's ashes lie beneath the tower, whose anteroom houses a collection of surfing artifacts that is regularly open to the public

Left and above left: Looking south (toward the Municipal Wharf) and north along the shore from near Santa Cruz's West Cliff Drive. Watersports enthusiasts will be keen to visit the Surfing Museum at the Mark Abbott Memorial Lighthouse (see panel).

1834; a modern replica of its chapel can be seen just around the corner from the State Park, at Emmet and School Streets.

To resume our journey, we go back along Mission to its junction with the Cabrillo Highway (Highway 1); the main road takes us across the San Lorenzo River and east to the edge of town.

CALIFORNIA

CALIFORNIA REPUBLIC

| San Francisco (Presidio) | **1431** | Pacifica | **1448** | Half Moon Bay | **1491** | Santa Cruz |
| **1419** | Daly City | **1439** | Moss Beach | **1453** | Davenport | **1503** |

Below: A trial run at the Laguna Seca Raceway, a few miles outside Monterey. Events held at the track raise substantial sums for local charities.

Highway 1, now transformed from a narrow coast road into a controlled access freeway, broadly follows the contours of Monterey Bay as it heads east and then south. Outside Santa Cruz, it passes the exit for Soquel, celebrated among counterculturalists as the site of the first Acid Test—a wild, LSD-driven gathering staged in November 1965 by novelist Ken Kesey's "Merry Pranksters." Other participants included poet Allen Ginsberg, and a then obscure San Francisco-based rock band named the Grateful Dead.

After a few more miles, the highway moves further away from the shore, and we take the exit from it marked "Seascape—San Andreas Road." This leads down towards the ocean, and a junction with a tree-lined sidetrack bringing us to Manresa

Above: The view from the Laguna Seca Raceway's stands. A string of national and international car and bike competitions takes place here every year.

Above: Manresa State Beach – reached via the San Andreas Road turnoff from Highway 1 about 11 miles south of Santa Cruz.

State Beach, a beauty spot also popular with surfers and kayakers. As we continue south, San Andreas is separated from Highway 1 by railroad tracks and wide expanses of strawberry fields; we eventually rejoin the freeway, via Beach Road, a little south of Watsonville.

The next towns we encounter are Moss Landing and Castroville; around them lies a mixture of marsh and arable land, and a succession of roadside billboards promoting the approaching attractions of Monterey. Soon, sand dunes become visible on our right, and the fields begin to give way to narrower patches of gorse, grass and scrub as we come closer to the sea. South of Seaside, we leave Highway 1 again, taking Routes 218 and 68 to one of this region's biggest sporting attractions, the Mazda Laguna Seca Raceway. Opened in 1957 on land originally leased from the nearby Fort Ord Army base, Laguna Seca (Spanish for "Dry Lagoon") is

run on a not-for-profit basis by the Sports Car Racing Association of the Monterey Peninsula. It hosts numerous major competitions, and on non-race days, visitors can drive around its perimeter for a clear, though sometimes distant view of the 2 ¼-mile track, stands and pits. From the Raceway entrance, turn right onto Route 68 for the last few miles of the journey to Monterey.

Left and below: Strawberrries being picked and packed in fields beside San Andreas Road. Their harvesting season in this region lasts from February to November.

Monterey's Waterfront

Above: Yachts and other small craft, seen from an observation deck on Monterey's Fisherman's Wharf.

Below: Monterey's Custom House, California's oldest public building, dates from 1827, and is open, free of charge, to visitors throughout the year.

Monterey's historic waterfront sites are easy to reach from the main highway: follow the signs for Fisherman's Wharf, and park at one of the lots near Custom House Plaza, as the surrounding area needs to be explored on foot.

Constructed in 1827 by the Mexican authorities, the adobe-and-stone Custom House was the collection point for taxes—some as high as 100%—on the port's incoming cargoes, as well as a potent symbol of foreign rule over the city. Accordingly, it was here that Commodore John Drake Sloat, sent to take Monterey by U.S. President James Polk, chose to raise the American flag on July 7, 1846, five days after entering the harbor onboard his ship, the *Savannah*. Sloat's bold proclamation, also issued on July 7, that "henceforward California will be a portion of the United States" proved a little premature (Mexico did not officially cede control over the state until 1848), but his subjugation of the city was a key strategic event; it also saw off

the British, who had had their own designs on Monterey and its surrounding region.

The Custom House remained in use until 1867, by which time Monterey had been supplanted as state capital by Sacramento, and had lost much of its seaborne trade to San Francisco. An initiative by the California-based Native Sons of the Golden

All three photographs below: The Fisherman's Wharf area is undeniably colorful and bustling — although the seabirds perching on the partially submerged rock just to the Wharf's northwest appear to prefer their rather more restful environment!

West led to the building's restoration in the early 1900s, and it later became the state's first officially recognized Historic Landmark.

Fisherman's Wharf, a few yards away, has been memorably described by author Ray Riegert as an example of "what the travel industry thinks tourists think a fishing pier should look like." It is a largely modern structure (nothing survives of its predecessor, designed by Thomas O. Larkin and opened in 1846) and most of its stores and amusements are predictably garish. However, it is worth investigating—not least for its observation decks, with their excellent views across the Bay and towards the nearby Municipal Wharf and marina.

Above: A relic of Monterey's seafaring past: this old, weatherbeaten anchor, now displayed near the Custom House, was salvaged from the Bay in 1944. Its precise age and origins are unknown.

Below: Monterey's Coast Guard Pier, seen from San Carlos Beach Park, close to the shoreline recreation trail that leads from the Fisherman's Wharf area toward Cannery Row.

The area around Custom House Plaza contains a number of important buildings, including California's first-ever theatre (on Pacific), and the house briefly occupied by the Scottish author and poet Robert Louis Stevenson at 530 Houston,

Below The premises at 800 Cannery Row that housed the laboratory of Ed 'Doc' Ricketts – a real-life marine biologist who appeared as a character in Steinbeck's novel about the area; and a mural on the Enterprise Cannery building, near the start of the Row.

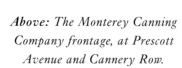

Above: The Monterey Canning Company frontage, at Prescott Avenue and Cannery Row.

between Pearl and Webster. For many tourists, though, Monterey's prime attraction is Cannery Row—the former heart of the city's sardine-packaging industry, immortalized in fiction by John Steinbeck (1902–1968). It lies northwest of Fisherman's Wharf, and is reached via a "recreation trail" that runs along the shoreline, past the Coast Guard Pier, and parallel to the Row itself.

Though called "Cannery Row" in Steinbeck's 1945 novel of the same name, this famous thoroughfare was originally known as Ocean View Avenue before being officially rechristened in 1953. The earliest canneries, established here at the end of the nineteenth century, produced tinned salmon; but by the early 1900s, an abundance of sardines in

Monterey Bay, together with better, faster processing methods, made the smaller fish more profitable. Within a few decades, sardine canning was a multi-million dollar business, eighteen factories were operating on Ocean View, and the surrounding district had become home to thousands of workers (many of them émigrés from Asia) and their families.

to examine the murals and carefully preserved workers' shacks further along the street. Nearby is a small tribute to John Steinbeck: a plaza bearing his name, adorned with a bronze bust.

Below: A sailor-suited monkey entertains visitors to Monterey's Custom House Plaza.

> **Cannery Row in Monterey in California is a poem, a stink, a grating noise, a quality of light, a tone, a habit, a nostalgia, a dream.**
>
> *John Steinbeck, Cannery Row, 1945*

Over-fishing led to a fall in the local sardine supply from the late 1940s onwards, and the last working cannery on the Row, the Hovden plant at its western end, closed down in 1972. However, this building was to play an important part in the neighborhood's renaissance. 1977 saw the start of an ambitious project (financed, to the tune of $55 million, by computer mogul David Packard) to convert it into a state-of-the-art aquarium, which opened, to widespread acclaim, in 1984. It currently attracts 1.8 million annual visitors, many of whom stay to sample the pleasures of a now-transformed Cannery Row's glossy restaurants and stores—and

California's Central Coast

The coastline beyond Monterey is characterized by transitions and contrasts, as the coiffed elegance of the scenic drive to Carmel gives way to the rugged magnificence of Big Sur. Here, we bid farewell to the redwoods that have been a part of the landscape for hundreds of miles: they are not found farther south. And, as we follow Highway 101 towards Santa Barbara and Ventura, we begin to encounter the dryer climate, vivid, lush flora and warm sunlight that will accompany us from here to Mexico.

Above: One of the bell towers atop Casa Grande at Hearst Castle — William Randolph Hearst's hilltop estate, designed by Julia Morgan, which attracts thousands of visitors each year.

California's Central Coast

"**V**ery few suspect that Californians have the best of us, and that, far from living in a kind of rude exile, they enjoy, in fact, the finest climate, the most fertile soil, the loveliest skies, the mildest winters, the most healthful region, in the whole United States." These words come from *California: For Health, Pleasure and Residence*, published in 1872. Its author, Charles Nordhoff (1830–1901), was a New York journalist who had traveled extensively in the Golden State, and was especially enamored of its Central Coast, to which his books and magazine articles attracted many settlers. Before completing his guide to California, he had written an influential essay for *Harper's Bazaar* extolling the beauties of Santa Barbara; and the town now called Ojai, north of Ventura, was originally named Nordhoff in his honor (he later praised the "abundance and loveliness" of its surrounding woodlands).

Nordhoff, whose own family went on to became longtime Santa Barbara residents, offered his readers not only purple prose, but valuable advice about farm crop selection, water supplies, road conditions, and other potentially troublesome subjects. However, those with deep enough pockets could easily solve almost any difficulty associated with living and doing business in remote, underdeveloped Western locations. Millionaire prospector and future California Senator George Hearst (1820–1891) bought up thousands of acres around San Simeon from the mid-1860s onwards—and, in the absence of railroad links, built his own wharf at the nearby harbor to transport materials for his mining and agricultural operations. His son, William Randolph Hearst (1863–1951), undaunted by the region's poor

Above: Ragged Point, a wonderful spot from which to observe the surrounding shoreline, lies about halfway between San Francisco and Los Angeles.

Below: The principal lobbyist for the building of the Pacific highway in this area was a local physician, John L. D. Roberts; his wishes were eventually fulfilled with its opening in 1937.

Above: The Hearst Castle grounds, and an elephant seal colony on a nearby beach.

highways, once rode down the coast to his father's San Simeon estate on horseback; and in 1919, he began to create his own dream home, Hearst Castle, there—a project that would have been inconceivable for anyone without his extraordinary combination of iron determination and vast wealth (see pages 130–133).

By the 1930s, Hearst was able to fly to and from San Simeon in a private airplane, and he undoubtedly relished the relative isolation of his "Enchanted Hill." For the less wealthy, transportation remained a serious problem until the inauguration of the coastal highway to Carmel. After more than two decades of campaigning, work on its construction started in 1922, and the road was finally completed in 1937. Twenty-eight years later, the then First Lady, Lady Bird Johnson, dedicated it as California's first scenic highway.

Above: The view north from a roadside turnout about 4 miles north of Lucia, showing the 500' long Big Creek Bridge. It was built in 1937, and has recently been renovated.

Below: Hearst Castle reflects its owner's taste for Spanish and Italian architecture.

Above: A trolley bus on San Luis Obispo's Higuera Street.
Below: Main Street (seen from Oak) in the elegant coastal town of Ventura.

Far right: Point Piños Lighthouse. Its bungalow-style base provided accommodation for its keepers; unusually, two women, Charlotte Layton and Emily Fish, were successively in charge of it during its early years.

The town of Pacific Grove lies just northwest of Monterey; David Avenue, which connects at right angles with Cannery Row and Lighthouse Avenue, marks the city limits between the two communities. Drive along Lighthouse, past the intersection with David, and then turn onto Ocean View Boulevard, which follows the shore.

This area, formerly known as Punta de Piños (Promontory of Pines), was once the property of a wealthy local landowner, David Jack—a Scottish émigré who had made good by selling guns in San

Above, and right: Sunset at Point Piños. The natural beauty of this area has attracted and inspired two distinguished authors: Robert Louis Stevenson (see quote panel); and, later, John Steinbeck, who lived and worked in the Pacific Grove cottage shown opposite between 1930-1936, and returned here frequently in later life.

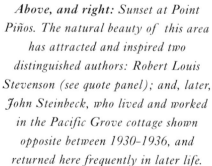

Francisco during the gold rush. In the 1870s, Jack permitted a Methodist minister, Reverend W.S. Ross, who had been in ailing health, to spend a few months camping in the woods near the sea. The mild climate and pleasant surroundings speeded Ross's recovery, and he went on to lead a successful campaign to found a Methodist summer camp in Punta de Piños. Jack agreed to provide the land for it at the bargain price of $1 an acre, and the first Pacific Grove Retreat took place in 1875. Conditions for attendees were Spartan and strict, with a dress code forbidding any unseemly display of buttocks or thighs while wearing swimsuits. The Methodists also banned alcohol from their "Christian Seaside Resort;" this prohibition was endorsed by the permanent residents of Pacific Grove when the town was incorporated in 1889, and it stayed in force for the next 80 years! Today, the Grove has a population of some 16,000: its agreeable environment attracts both human visitors, and the colonies of rare Monarch butterflies that spend every winter here.

> **The Pacific booms in front. Westward is Point Piños, with the lighthouse in a wilderness of sand… To the east, and still nearer, you will come upon a space of open down, a hamlet, a haven among rocks, a world of surge and screaming seagulls.**
>
> *Robert Louis Stevenson, "The Woods and the Pacific,"*
> *from* **Across the Plains** *(1879)*

Left: Lovers' Point Park, adorned with a carpet of seasonal wild flowers, viewed from near Ocean Park Boulevard in Pacific Grove.

A little further along the highway, we reach Point Piños—site of the oldest West Coast lighthouse still in operation. It dates from 1855 (Lighthouse Avenue was originally constructed as a route for its supplies), and continues to use its original Fresnel lens (see pages 52–53), although it is now powered by electricity instead of the sperm whale oil it previously ran on.

Pacific Grove	1557	Point Joe	1561	Lone Cypress	1565	17-mile drive exit

CALIFORNIA
CALIFORNIA REPUBLIC

1554 | 17-mile drive entrance | 1559 | Fanshell Overlook | 1563 | Lodge at Pebble Beach | 1568

Below: Bird Rock provides an ideal habitat for gulls, cormorants, and numerous other avian species. Sea lions and seals can also be seen there.

Beyond Lighthouse Avenue (just south of Point Piños), the road nearest the ocean becomes Sunset Drive. We follow it round past Asilomar State Beach—once the property of the YWCA, which held a competition to name it in 1913; the winning entry, submitted by a Stanford University student, combined the Greek word for "refuge" and the Spanish *mar* (sea)—and towards the Pacific Grove tollgate for the famous 17-mile Pebble Beach scenic drive.

The land through which this privately owned route passes originally belonged, like Pacific Grove, to David Jack (see previous two pages). He sold it in 1880 to a group of entrepreneurs who created a pay-for-access carriage road and, later, the Del Monte golf links there. Since then, other thriving sports and leisure facilities have been established nearby—including the Pebble Beach golf course, which regularly hosts major championships, and has been rated "America's finest" by *Golf Digest* magazine. However, the area's most outstanding attractions are its landscapes and beaches, whose excellence more than justifies the entrance fee (currently $8).

Above and left: The land and the shore near Point Joe; and a photograph taken a little farther down the scenic drive, looking toward Fanshell Overlook.

Navigating the scenic drive is easy: visitors are handed a map as they enter, and all places of interest on the route are clearly signposted and numbered. First, we head down to Point Joe, a promontory surrounded by dangerous rocks and turbulent currents. In the sea beyond it lie the submerged remains of numerous ships that came too close—or

were wrecked after their navigators mistook this coastline for Monterey Bay. As we continue south near the water's edge, the Spyglass Hill Golf Course (opened in 1966, and named for a location in Robert Louis Stevenson's *Treasure Island*) can be seen to our left. For a superb view of the adjacent shore, go to Fanshell Overlook: fanshells, sometimes found on the beach beneath, are a rare species of clam, but these sands are best known as the pupping grounds for the harbor seals (the Pacific coast's most ubiquitous marine mammals) who come here every spring to give birth.

Above: The beach northeast of Point Joe on the 17-mile scenic drive.

121

Below and right: Perhaps the most famous single tree anywhere on this coastline, the Lone Cypress has withstood the onslaughts of the elements for more than two centuries, and continues to flourish on its precarious oceanside perch.

Southwest of the Fanshell Overlook, the road begins to climb, entering the woods as it approaches the most famous landmark on the 17-mile scenic drive: the 250-year old Lone Cypress. This is a weather-beaten but still hardy specimen of *cupressus macrocarpa* (the Monterey cypress), a once-endangered breed of tree which occurs naturally only here and at Point Lobos, south of Carmel. It has survived not just the Pacific winds but also an arson attack in 1984, and has become so symbolic of the surrounding region that it has been adopted as a trademark by the Pebble Beach Company, owners of the drive and much of its adjacent land. Nearby stands a plaque commemorating Samuel F.B. Morse (1885–1969), who founded the company in 1919, and was responsible not only for masterminding the development of its golf courses and other amenities, but also for safeguarding their unique natural setting.

Left The beach (surprisingly quiet for such a sunny day!) at the bottom of Ocean Avenue in Carmel-by-the-Sea. Across the bay is the area we have just passed through on the scenic drive.

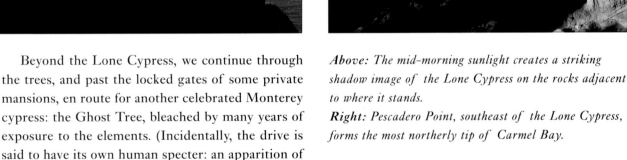

Beyond the Lone Cypress, we continue through the trees, and past the locked gates of some private mansions, en route for another celebrated Monterey cypress: the Ghost Tree, bleached by many years of exposure to the elements. (Incidentally, the drive is said to have its own human specter: an apparition of a lady in white lace, seen wandering the road at night.) A little further along the coast, we encounter Pescadero Point—a delightful spot, offering views across Carmel Bay and Stillwater Cove, (which lies just to its east), and populated by squirrels and other usually timid creatures that have become surprisingly accustomed to visitors!

The Pebble Beach golf links occupy the land closest to the Cove; the road passes the entrance to

Above: The mid-morning sunlight creates a striking shadow image of the Lone Cypress on the rocks adjacent to where it stands.
Right: Pescadero Point, southeast of the Lone Cypress, forms the most northerly tip of Carmel Bay.

its Lodge, built by Samuel Morse in 1919, before reaching the Carmel tollgate leading back to Highway 1. Some travelers may wish to stay on the scenic drive as it snakes through the Del Monte Forest and around the Poppy Hills golf course to the north; but we now exit onto San Antonio Street, which takes us to a junction with Ocean Avenue. To our right is the beach; to our left the route into downtown Carmel.

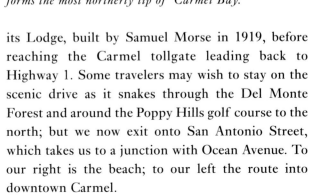

123

Below: An old sign on the outside wall of a building at Ocean Avenue and Mission Street in Carmel, now occupied by an furniture store.

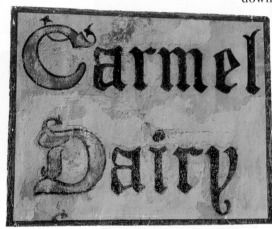

Below and right: Carmel's Village Inn, at Junipero and Ocean; and the Tuck Box tearoom, whose quaintly charming premises date from the 1920s.

Carmel-by-the-Sea (to give the city its full name) is a bijou bayside community whose narrow streets can scarcely contain the flood of tourists they frequently attract. A walk around its picturesque downtown area is undoubtedly enjoyable—though visitors may find that parking restrictions limit the time they can spend there! Follow Ocean Avenue east from the beach towards the stores, restaurants and galleries that form the heart of modern Carmel: the district settled by the eighteenth century Spanish padres who built the Mission San Carlos Borromeo de Carmelo lies a little to the south, and is featured on the next two pages.

The town took shape in the 1900s, when businessman James Franklin Devendorf, the owner of a nearby hotel, began to encourage artists and writers to make their homes on land provided by the

Carmel Development Company, which he ran in partnership with Frank H. Powers. Early arrivals included poet George Sterling, author Mary Austin, and (briefly) novelist and essayist Jack London—who, in his *Valley of The Moon* (1913), recorded his first impressions of the little village's "pungent pines… [and] woods-embowered cottages, quaint and rustic."

Such idyllic surroundings soon became highly sought after; and, with the arrival of wealthier homebuyers, prices rose, and the original residents (some of whose bohemian lifestyles had gone down badly with their new neighbors) were gradually forced out. Nevertheless, community leaders strove to retain as much as possible of Carmel's unspoiled character, passing an ordinance in 1929 determining that "business and commerce have in the past, are now, and are proposed to be in the future subordinated to [the city's] residential character."

This legislation has had an enduring effect. Ugly modern storefronts are not permitted in Carmel

(neither, curiously, are street numbers), and the town displays an immaculately groomed prettiness that some critics find artificial and cloying. However, most tourists find it hard not to succumb to the gingerbread-house charm of The Tuck Box tearoom (on Dolores between Ocean and 7th), or to the agreeably "old-world" flavor of many other nearby buildings.

Above: The natural glory of Carmel's bayside forms a piquant contrast with the town's more stylized central area.

Above: Tourists mingle with Sunday worshippers at the Mission San Carlos Borromeo de Carmelo. The building has been memorably described by one architectural historian as "the romantic gem of the California chain."

Carmel's Mission can be reached by driving along Santa Lucia Avenue (at the southern end of the town), and turning right onto Rio. The second of the religious communities created by the colonizing and evangelizing group of Franciscan priests led by Father Junípero Serra, it dates from 1771—although the buildings housing it were not completed until some twenty-six years later.

Monterey had been the original site chosen for a Mission in this region (see pages 98–99); relocation to Carmel was largely prompted by the area's more fertile land, and the presence of a substantial native population which could be converted to Christianity and pressed into labor. Serra made the new settlement his headquarters (though his duties as Father-President of the steadily expanding chain of Californian missions meant that he was often absent), and by the early 1780s, was supervising plans to replace its existing adobe chapel with a more permanent stone structure.

Sadly, Serra never witnessed its completion. He died on August 28, 1784, and was buried, alongside another veteran of the "Sacred Expedition" of 1769, Father Juan Crespi (see pages 94–95), in the

1588 Point Sur

Ripplewood Resort

1596

1599

Big Sur (Post Office)

1619

Lucia

Sand Dollar Beach

1629

1644

Ragged Point

San Simeon

1660

Cambria

1668

old Carmel chapel. Fermín Francisco de Lasuén, who was appointed Father-President in 1785, oversaw the construction of the current church, and the Mission San Carlos flourished and expanded during his years in charge. However, after his death in 1803, Santa Barbara was made the administrative center for the Californian missions, and over the next few decades, the Carmel settlement's fortunes declined steadily. Following secularization in 1834, it was abandoned, and eventually became derelict.

The church was re-roofed in 1884, but more extensive restoration work did not begin until the 1930s. Its success enabled the Mission to be used as a parish church from 1933 onwards; it was raised to the status of a Basilica in 1961, and is now both a center for local worship and a popular destination for visitors. The Vatican beatified Father Serra, its founder, in 1988.

Below: A view of the area to the right of the church. The building standing among the trees and hedges is a museum named for its first curator, Harry Downie (1903–1980), who played a key role in restoring the Mission site.

Below: Looking north across Carmel Bay from near the corner of Scenic Road and San Antonio Street.

Below: Bixby Bridge spans 320 feet, and was completed in 1932, five years before the opening of this section of the Pacific Coast Highway.
Bottom: Sand Dollar Beach is named for the tiny, coin-shaped sea-urchins often found there.

Right (main picture): The dramatic coastline of Big Sur stretches from here to San Simeon; Point Sur can be seen at the top right of the photo.

On leaving the Carmel Mission, we follow Rio to Highway 1, which now heads towards Big Sur—the famous section of Pacific coast whose name derives from the Spanish phrase *"el sur grande"* ("the big [country to the] south"). Its majestic landscape is dominated by redwood forests and steep, sometimes sheer cliffs and slopes; after covering ten miles or so, pull over and look back at the seemingly endless chain of headlands stretching away to the north. There are also impressive sights closer to hand, like the view—best avoided by vertigo sufferers!—from the northern edge of Bixby Bridge (13 miles south of Carmel) to the creek bed 265 feet below.

Soon, the rocky outcrop of Point Sur appears to our right. On its slopes stands a lighthouse that has been in operation here since 1889 (unfortunately, it can only be visited by prior arrangement: see pages 188–189). Beyond the Point, Highway 1 moves slightly inland, and descends into the leafy shade of the Big Sur Valley, passing the stores and cabins of Ripplewood Resort before starting to climb again. There are no signs to mark our arrival in the village of Big Sur, though we pass its Post Office three miles from Ripplewood. A little to the south lie the gates of the library opened in 1981 to commemorate novelist Henry Miller (1891–1980), one of several distinguished writers and artists who made their homes in this area from the 1940s onwards.

The road twists and undulates through the next few miles, but eventually resumes its course near the ocean—running closer to sea level than before, with little or no shoulder between the pavement and the cliff's edge in many places. Nine miles south of Lucia, we reach Sand Dollar Beach—a favorite

> ❝ Big Sur has a climate of its own and a character all its own. It is a region where extremes meet, a region where one is always conscious of weather, of space, of grandeur, and of eloquent silence. ❞
>
> *Henry Miller,* Big Sur and the Oranges of Hieronymus Bosch, *1957*

location for both surfers and hang-gliding enthusiasts—and continue to Ragged Point, a rocky peninsula that has been a popular rest stop for travelers on Highway 1 since the 1950s, and now boasts a successful hotel and other tourist facilities.

Above: The view north up the coast from the viewing platform at the tip of Ragged Point.

129

Hearst Castle

Below: A glimpse of Hearst Castle and its surrounding landscape from the winding road linking the 'Enchanted Hill' to the Visitor Center some 1,600 feet below.

Above: House C, 'Casa del Sol' - one of the three guesthouses that surround the Castle's Casa Grande.

Far right: Casa Grande, seen from the Enchanted Hill's Central Plaza. The 'four-leaf' pool contains the statue Galatea on a Dolphin, *by Italian sculptor Leopoldo Ansiglioni.*

Our first glimpse of Hearst Castle from Highway 1 creates an unforgettable impression. Seen from a distance, its gleaming towers and tiled roofs have a mirage-like quality, rendered even more magical by the swirling mists that sometimes obscure the hillside below them. Few travelers will want to miss the chance of taking a closer look at this truly extraordinary place.

Guided tours of what is officially known as the Hearst San Simeon State Historical Monument begin at its Visitor Center, about 15 miles from Ragged Point; from here, we travel the 5 miles to the Castle itself by coach. Designed for William Randolph Hearst (1863–1951) by architect Julia Morgan (see side panel), it took 28 years to build. Hearst's initial plans in 1919 were for "a little something" to replace the tents then being used for accommodation at his San Simeon ranch; but his dream developed into a commission for an elegant, opulent estate, centered around a magnificent mansion ("Casa Grande"), and boasting three guest houses, two swimming pools, gardens, terraces, and even a zoo.

The slow pace of construction at what Hearst named "La Cuesta Encantada" (the "Enchanted Hill") was largely due to his own interventions and changes of mind over the plans—though there were also considerable problems with the supply and transportation of raw materials to its high, remote site. According to author Victoria Kastner, early hopes of concluding the entire project by 1921 were soon abandoned, and the first of the guest houses (House A—"Casa del Mar") was not ready for occupation until 1923. After the completion of Houses B and C, and the opening of the outdoor, 345,000-gallon Neptune Pool, work focused on Casa Grande; this was in use by the middle of the decade, but underwent numerous modifications over the following years. Julia Morgan's later additions to the Castle included the indoor Roman Pool, the North

Photos courtesy of Hearst Castle/California State Parks

Julia Morgan

Julia Morgan (1872–1957) was the most distinguished female American architect of her generation. Born in San Francisco, she graduated in civil engineering from the University of California at Berkeley in 1894; there she met the influential architect and teacher Bernard Maybeck, who encouraged her to study at the École des Beaux-Arts in Paris, which he himself had attended. Morgan's five-year stay in France was partially financed by William Randoph Hearst's mother, Phoebe Apperson Hearst. Mrs. Hearst, an admirer and patron of Maybeck's work, provided similar support to a number of his other students, and later endowed a scholarship program at the University of California.

After becoming the first woman to receive a certificate in architecture from the École, Morgan returned to the Bay Area, and spent three years as an employee of architect John Galen Howard, during which she was involved with several commissions for the Hearst family. She set up her own practice in 1905, and designed a wide range of college, church, domestic and public buildings—many of them reflecting her fascination with Spanish, Italian and Chinese styles. Though Hearst Castle was to occupy much of her later career, she continued to work on numerous other projects (mostly in California), until declining health forced her retirement in the mid-1940s.

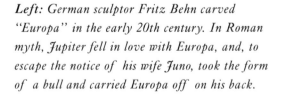

Left: German sculptor Fritz Behn carved "Europa" in the early 20th century. In Roman myth, Jupiter fell in love with Europa, and, to escape the notice of his wife Juno, took the form of a bull and carried Europa off on his back.

Wing, and the expanded Celestial Suite. Her involvement with San Simeon continued until 1945, the year in which she submitted her final costings for the creation of "La Cuesta Encantada," totaling $4,717,000.

131

Above: "The Wrestlers", outside "Casa del Monte." A copy, by the Romanelli Brothers, of an ancient Roman sculpture in the Uffizi Gallery in Florence.

Below: Decorative carvings above Casa Grande's main doorway include a medieval statue of the Virgin Mary.

Hearst Castle's buildings, and the exquisite artifacts displayed in its rooms and gardens, reflect the eclectic tastes of its owner. "The Ranch," as William Randolph Hearst often referred to his San Simeon estate, was conceived at least partly as a showcase for the *objets d'art* he had collected assiduously from his earliest years; and its overall design borrows liberally from Classical and Spanish traditions, creating skilful reworkings and syntheses of the architecture he had admired on his European travels. A few of the ingredients of this rich stylistic mix come from even farther afield, such as the carvings of the Egyptian goddess Sekhmet (an attendant of the sun god Ra) displayed on the South Esplanade; these are the oldest statues in the collection, dating from between 2000 and 1550 B.C.

Although Hearst envisioned his castle as a "museum," it had other more worldly and practical functions. From the mid-1920s until the late 40s, he and his companion, actress Marion Davies (1897–1961) spent much of their time there; and his study, in Casa Grande's Gothic Suite, became the place from which he supervised his newspapers and business interests. The Ranch was also where Hearst did his entertaining:

guests at his lavish house parties included showbusiness stars (Charlie Chaplin, Greta Garbo, Clark Gable), writers, artists, and distinguished politicians such as former U.S. President Calvin Coolidge and future British Prime Minister

Above: A 3rd century A.D. Roman sarcophagus on the North Esplanade. Among the deities it portrays are the Muses—goddesses associated with the arts. Left: The main doorway to House C.

Winston Churchill. During the day, visitors could relax around the Castle's grounds, and enjoy its sports and leisure facilities; in the evening, they were joined by their host for dinner in Casa Grande's Refectory.

Hearst remained devoted to "La Cuesta Encantada"—but in 1947, his increasingly precarious health forced him to leave it for Los Angeles. Six years after his death, the Hearst Corporation donated the Castle to the State of California; it was opened to the public in 1958, and was declared a National Historical Landmark in 1976. Five tours are available, and Hearst Castle is open 362 days a year.

Above left: Looking up from the West Terrace towards the west front of House C.
Above top: The South Terrace, with a 16th century marble wellhead.
Above: "The Three Graces" (a copy of Italian sculptor Antonio Canova's original) in the Castle grounds.

![California Republic flag]

CALIFORNIA

| 1629 | Ragged Point | 1660 | Cambria | 1684 | Morro Bay | 1704 |
| Sand Dollar Beach | 1644 | San Simeon | 1668 | Cayucos | 1690 | San Luis Obispo |

Cholame

Above and below: James Dean, whose love of fast cars was to prove fatal; and the memorial to him in Cholame. Part of its inscription reads: "The petals of early spring always fall at the height of their ephemeral brilliance."

So far, we have succeeded in avoiding excessive deviations from the Pacific Coast road, but we now make a rare exception to this rule by taking a sidetrip to Cholame—the dusty little town, some 50 miles inland, where movie star James Dean met his death in a road accident on September 30, 1955, at the age of only 24.

To get there, we turn onto Route 46 13 miles beyond San Simeon, and continue towards its junction with 101. Here, we take the main road north for a few miles, before heading east again on 46 near Paso Robles, and driving across the bare, dreary landscape of the Coast Ranges to our destination. Cholame itself is little more than a cluster of buildings, and its only prominent feature is the memorial to Dean erected in 1977 (with additions in 1983) by a Japanese businessman, Seita Ohnishi. Two slabs beside the striking, though sadly vandalized artwork carry a dedication, and a statement from Mr. Ohnishi: "This monument stands as a small token of my appreciation of the people of America." The steel sculpture bears a brief quotation from the star's favorite story, *The Little Prince* by Antoine de Saint-Exupéry: "What is essential is invisible to the eye."

Dean was killed a little to the east of the monument, at the intersection between Routes 46 and 41. He had been traveling west on 46 (then known as 466) in his recently acquired silver Porsche (see panel), and had already picked up a citation for speeding prior to reaching the Cholame junction, which he approached at about 85 miles per hour. There, he collided with an oncoming vehicle driven by a local man, Donald Turnupseed, who subsequently stated that he never saw the other car. Both Turnupseed and Dean's passenger, motor mechanic Rolf Wütherich, escaped with minor injuries; Dean was later pronounced dead in hospital at Paso Robles.

"Please, never get in it"

The week before his death, James Dean had a chance meeting at a Los Angeles restaurant with the distinguished English actor Sir Alec Guinness (1914–2000). In his autobiography, Blessings in Disguise, *Guinness recalls that Dean took him to a nearby parking lot to show him his new Porsche Spyder sports car, which he had not yet driven. Guinness's reaction was unexpected and disturbing: he found himself "saying in a voice I could hardly recognize as my own, 'Please, never get in it... It is now ten o'clock, Friday the 23rd of September, 1955. If you get in that car you will be found dead in it by this time next week.'" Dean laughed, told Guinness "not to be so mean," and the incident was quickly brushed aside; but the Englishman's strange moment of prescience proved to be all too accurate.*

Left and below: *The junction of Routes 46 and 41, where James Dean met his death (the roads here have been remade since the 1950s).*

Right: *A floral tribute from a fan nestles inside Seita Ohnishi's James Dean commemoration.*

Wildlife

Below: A juvenile gopher snake seen on the Earthquake Trail at the Bear Valley Visitor Center, Olema, CA.

A significant proportion of Pacific Coast Highway travelers are wildlife lovers; and a certain camaraderie (combined, perhaps, with a little friendly rivalry) can develop between the enthusiasts who find themselves thrown together at successive vista points and overlooks. They brandish their telephoto lenses and powerful binoculars in the hope of sighting a rare or shy bird or animal—and their persistence is frequently rewarded, as the road has

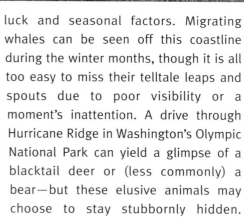

Above: A group of pelicans take a rest between their fishing expeditions near Pismo Beach, CA .

done remarkably little to disrupt the habitats and behavior of the creatures that live beside it.

Nevertheless, wildlife watching in these conditions is often dependent on a combination of luck and seasonal factors. Migrating whales can be seen off this coastline during the winter months, though it is all too easy to miss their telltale leaps and spouts due to poor visibility or a moment's inattention. A drive through Hurricane Ridge in Washington's Olympic National Park can yield a glimpse of a blacktail deer or (less commonly) a bear—but these elusive animals may choose to stay stubbornly hidden. However, at other times, fortune can smile on the most casual of observers: the elk photograph above was taken within yards of the highway at an apparently unpromising Northern Californian site.

Above : Human spectators have little impact on this impressive male elk and his female companions, pictured near Lady Bird Johnson Grove, CA.

For tourists who want to see as much fauna as possible, but have limited time in which to do so, locations where large numbers of creatures congregate will probably provide the most satisfaction. These include the numerous sea lion colonies we have already encountered along the coast, as well as the 7,000-strong group of elephant seals on the beach some 4 miles south of Hearst Castle. Bird-watchers will find no shortage of seaside vantage points in this region (Pismo Beach is one of many places where pelicans can be observed hunting for prey); and it is also worth keeping an eye on roadside pastures for occasional curiosities among farm-bred animals—like the zebra (descendants of those originally brought here by William Randolph Hearst) grazing alongside the cattle near San Simeon!

Above and top: Sea lion and seal colonies are quite common on the rocky shores of Oregon and California. The top picture was taken at Heceta Head, OR; the one beneath it at Piedras Blancas beach, near San Simeon, CA.

★ CALIFORNIA REPUBLIC
CALIFORNIA

1629 | Ragged Point | 1660 | Cambria | 1684 | Morro Bay | 1704
Sand Dollar Beach | 1644 | San Simeon | 1668 | Cayucos | 1690 | San Luis Obispo

Below: Regular trolley bus services provide an inexpensive and convenient way of getting around in San Luis Obispo.

Above and right: The front and back of the SLO Brewpub and Restaurant, 1119 Garden Street, San Luis Obispo. Originally a small-scale microbrewery, the company now markets its beers all over the West Coast – and beyond.

After taking in the glories of Hearst Castle, visitors may wish to relax for a while in the peaceful surroundings of the William Randolph Hearst Memorial State Beach, whose entrance is just opposite the Castle drive. With its flowering trees, picnic tables and fishing pier, it is an agreeable and restful spot—though the cove on which it lies acquired a more menacing character when it served as a location in Arnold Schwarzenegger's 1987 movie *Predator*.

From the Memorial Beach, Highway 1 leads south past the towns of San Simeon, Cambria and the junction with Route 46 (see preceding pages), heading toward Morro Bay and the looming offshore mass of its most famous landmark, Morro Rock. The harbor here, first charted in the 16th century, was a regular anchorage for Spanish and Mexican ships, while the town of Morro Bay, which dates from the 1870s, went on to become a center for fishing and tourism. It has also benefited (financially, if not aesthetically) from the setting up, in 1953, of the Pacific Gas & Electric power plant whose triple smokestacks dominate its skyline.

Beyond Morro Bay, we turn inland for the 14 mile journey to San Luis Obispo; perhaps the only really striking visual feature of this section of the highway is the huge American eagle symbol displayed on a hillside near the National Guard and military base a few miles north of the town. San Luis Obispo itself, the county seat of the region, owes its existence to the Mission established there by the tireless Father Junípero Serra in 1772. Its original chapel and cloisters burned down within a few years of their construction, but a restored version of the building that replaced them in the early 1790s can be found at the heart of the city's downtown area, on the corner of Monterey and Chorro Streets (Highway 1/Santa Rosa Street intersects with Monterey a few blocks away). Other nearby sites of interest include the County Historical Museum at Mission Plaza, and tthe award-winning SLO Brewpub and Restaurant on Garden Street, opened in 1988, and still run by its co-founders, Michael and Becky Hoffman.

Above: The Mission San Luis Obispo de Tolosa, downtown at Monterey and Chorro Streets, was the fifth to be built in California.

Above left: Colorful flora at the William Randolph Hearst State Beach, below the Castle's 'Enchanted Hill.'

Center inset: Looking across to Morro Rock from near Marina Square in Morro Bay.

Left: Afternoon sun and shade in the center of San Luis Obispo.

CALIFORNIA REPUBLIC

CALIFORNIA

1629 Sand Dollar Beach
Ragged Point
1644
1660 San Simeon
Cambria
1668
1684 Cayucos
Morro Bay
1690
1704 San Luis Obispo

Below: Vegetable crops being gathered and loaded beside Highway 1, just south of Guadalupe.

Below: Looking south along Pismo Beach (and on toward Grover Beach and Oceano) from a hotel gazebo off the town's Prince Street.

At San Luis Obispo, Highways 1 and 101 merge briefly. We rejoin them on the western edge of town, and follow them to their junction with Madonna Road, which leads to one of this area's best-loved landmarks, the Madonna Inn. Opened in 1958, it was named for its founders, Alex and Phyllis Madonna, who were jointly responsible for its extra-ordinary design and decor, and are still its managers. Each of the inn's 108 bedrooms has its own special theme and color scheme (favored materials include leopard and zebra skin fabrics and hand-carved stone), and its pink-and-gold dining room, Silver Bar and Copper Café are a perfect antidote to the uniformity of most American hotels.

Back on the main route south, we head for Pismo Beach, about 8 miles from here. The little resort has been popular with vacationers (and especially fishermen) since the 1890s, when the Southern

Pacific railroad established a depot nearby; as we enter the town, Highway 1 diverges from 101, and runs close to the shore. Soon, Pismo merges almost imperceptibly with the neighboring seafront settlement of Grover Beach; just beyond them lies Oceano, whose impressive sand dunes are easily accessible from the road.

For much of the last few hundred miles, we have passed through regions of outstanding scenic beauty and considerable affluence. However, as we move inland south of Oceano, a different aspect of Central California presents itself—and vacant lots, warehouses and seedy-looking stores give way to wide, drab expanses of fields growing lettuce, strawberries and similar produce. Most of the workers tending them live in communities like Guadalupe, the next

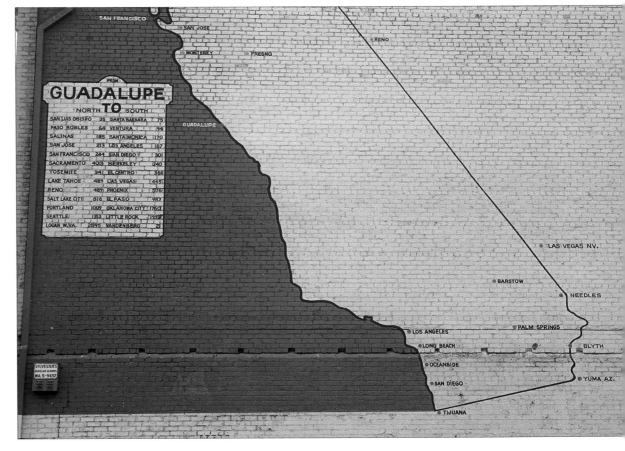

Above: The view from Pismo Beach's Eldwayen Ocean Park (at Ocean Boulevard and Montecito). Above right and right: The famous Madonna Inn, 100 Madonna Road, San Luis Obispo; and the downtown mural (see opposite) in Guadalupe.

sizeable place on our route. Though it boasts a busy Amtrak depot, Guadalupe's main drag has a shabby, outdated appearance. A large, faded mural, listing a selection of American cities and their distances from the town, prompts the unkind thought that many of its residents would prefer to be elsewhere, while the presence of a sizeable cemetery near its southern limits adds to the overall atmosphere of depression.

Below: The lavandería *outside the Mission Santa Bárbara. Its distinctive 'mountain lion' spout may be California's oldest public sculpture.*

Below: Avila Beach lies off the path of the main Pacific Coast highway, a few miles west of Pismo Beach.

Near Orcutt, southeast of Guadalupe, Highway 1 combines with Route 135 for a few miles, then splits off towards Lompoc. Before approaching it, we pass the entrance to Vandenberg Airforce Base—founded (as an Army training center, Camp Cooke) in 1941, renamed in 1958, and now a major launch site for missiles and satellites. The base has given a dramatic boost to the size and prosperity of Lompoc, whose population has risen from below 7,000 to over 58,000 in the last four decades. The town was originally best known for its commercial flower growing; this is still a significant local activity, and in spring, many of the fields surrounding the town are filled with colorful blooms.

Highway 1 enters Lompoc on H Street (north of downtown, it intersects with Purisima Road, the route to the Mission La Purísima Concepción, a few miles to the east), and continues down Ocean Avenue before turning south. Just over 20 miles from here, we connect with 101 and begin our progress along the southern Californian coast; but prior to embarking on this new stage of our journey, we take a short sidetrip west to Jalama Beach. The backroad

Above: Looking north along the line used by Amtrak coastal trains at the Jalama Beach railroad crossing.

leading there from Highway 1 is about 7 miles from Lompoc, and its narrow pavement twists and turns through a succession of hills and valleys on its 14-mile route to the shore. In places, the ocean appears tantalizingly in front of us, only to vanish as we

| Pismo Beach | 1704 | Oceano | 1728 | Lompoc | 1768 | Santa Barbara | 1842 |
| 1712 | Grover Beach | 1715 | Guadalupe | 1760 | Turnoff for Jalama Beach | 1815 | Ventura |

Jalama Beach

Left: Jalama Beach: though getting here involves a substantial detour from the main road, this shoreline is a favorite with surfers and whale-watchers.

church, completed in 1820, has been extensively rebuilt, but the site also contains earlier artifacts—including the exterior 'lavandería' (basin for clothes washing) constructed by Native American neophytes in 1808.

negotiate yet another bend—but on our arrival, we are rewarded by the sight of a long, sandy stretch of bay, popular with campers and windsurfers, but often pleasantly deserted.

We now double back to Highway 1, which joins 101 near Las Cruces. Santa Barbara is some 30 miles away; after reaching it, we exit onto Mission Street, and head for the Mission Santa Bárbara, established there by Father Fermin Lasuén in 1786. Its present

Above left and top: The Mission Santa Bárbara, 2201 Laguna Street. Like many other historic missions, it is now the center of a busy Catholic parish.

Above: This mural, by A. Mortimer, appears on the sidewall of Lompoc's Old Town Antique Mall, at Ocean Avenue and H Street.

Below and bottom: Santa Barbara's Shoreline Park (seen near Shoreline Drive and La Marina); and Shoreline Drive itself.

After its years as a Mission settlement, Santa Barbara prospered and expanded, attracting visitors and residents who arrived by stage-coach (a service from San Francisco was inaugurated in 1861) and later by railroad. In 1901, the city acquired one of its most distinctive features when its first palm trees were planted; and its restful atmosphere and mild, healthful climate have proved perennially attractive to well-heeled vacationers and retirees. It is also a focus for business and enterprise: the seeds of its current prominence in high-technology design and manu-facturing were sown as early as 1916, when brothers Malcolm and Allan Lockheed launched their pioneering airplane building company here.

The city's success is reflected in its elegant downtown area, a little to the east of the Mission. However, to explore its equally rewarding waterfront, head back to 101, turn right (north), and continue as far as the junction with Route 225 (Las Positas Road). Exit here, follow 225 down towards the ocean, turn left onto Cliff Drive, and then take a right onto Shoreline Drive, which leads down to the colorful Yacht Harbor. Beyond it, the road becomes Cabrillo Boulevard, and runs along the shore past Stearns Wharf—built in 1872, and the oldest structure of its kind in California.

From the Wharf, follow the signs to return to 101 South, which takes us on to Ventura. To our right is the Pacific; to our left, houses and other buildings perch above the highway, with receding tiers of hills and mountains (the San Rafael range and the more distant Sierra Madres) behind them. At Ventura, we turn off the main road at Figueroa Street, and quickly reach a junction with Main, and the Mission San Buenaventura. Dating from 1782, this was the last of the nine Missions founded by Father Junípero Serra; its church suffered serious earthquake damage in 1812, but has survived relatively unscathed since then. Just across the street, at 204 Main, the remains of the Mission's lavandería (see preceding pages) are buried beneath what is now a grocery store.

Above: East Main Street on Ventura, seen from near the junction with Califonia.

Left: Ventura's Mission San Buenaventura was named for a 13th century, Italian-born cardinal who became head of the Franciscan order.

The
Los Angeles Area

To its detractors, Los Angeles is synonymous with urban sprawl, pollution and traffic congestion, but our route through the city shows it at its most picturesque and exhilarating. As we journey from Malibu to Laguna, we encounter a succession of colorful beachfront communities, most of which are on (or fairly near) the path of Highway 1 as it heads southwest. Each has its own distinctive character and heritage—and, sometimes, a parallel existence as a movie or TV show location, or the subject of a song.

Above: A millionaires' row of dream homes by the ocean…beachfront houses near Malibu.

The Los Angeles Area

Above: The Warner Brothers (Harry, Sam, Albert, and Jack) arrived on the West Coast in 1923, when they founded their famous movie studio in Burbank.

The conquistador Juan Rodríguez Cabrillo (1498–1543) was probably the first European to set eyes on what is now the Los Angeles area. He had begun a voyage of discovery from Nueva España in Summer 1542, and, by September, had reached San Diego Bay (which he named San Miguel) and claimed it for Spain. According to subsequent accounts, Cabrillo considered the Bay "a sheltered port and a very good one," but he was less impressed with the smaller harbor—almost certainly San Pedro Bay—that he encountered farther up the coast a few weeks afterwards. Smoke from fires lit near the shore by its residents led to Cabrillo christening it "La Bahia de la Fumos" (the Bay of Fumes); deterred by this primitive example of Southern Californian smog, he declined to anchor there, preferring to press on toward what would later become Ventura.

Permanent Spanish occupation of the region began with the founding of the Mission San Gabriel Arcángel (a little to the northeast of modern downtown LA) in 1771. Ten years later, a small group of Mexican colonists, enticed by subsidies and the promise of land grants, set up a riverside *pueblo* (village) a few miles away, with support and protection from the Mission. Named for "Our Lady the Queen of the Angels" (Nuestra Señora la Reina de los Angeles), its population and productivity grew quickly; by 1800, according to historian John Walton Caughey, its agricultural output was second only to that of San Gabriel itself.

The Mission's resources were dissipated after its secularization in 1834; however, its loss proved to be Los Angeles' gain, and during the last few years of Mexican rule, the town once derided by the padres as a haunt of "idlers and gamblers" briefly became the

Below: The Wayfarers' Chapel on Palos Verdes Drive, Rancho Palos Verdes. Its designer was Lloyd Wright (son of Frank Lloyd Wright).

Right: The 'Pacific Wheel' – one of the many exciting rides on offer at the funfair on Santa Monica pier.

Left: This vintage flyer presents a typically idyllic image of beachside life.

capital of California. In the second half of the nineteenth century, it benefited, like the rest of the state, from an influx of new settlers—some brought West by the transcontinental railroad that arrived here in 1876; while the decision, taken in 1899, to construct a deep-water harbor at San Pedro was to make LA a center for international trade and transportation that would eventually rival even New York.

The city's love affair with the automobile began early. Cars were being made and driven here in the 1890s, and the Automobile Club of Southern California, formed in 1900, was soon producing maps and lobbying for better roads. By the early 1920s, work had begun on a coastal highway, which was completed by the end of the decade; initially named the Roosevelt Highway, it was subsequently redesignated Highway 3, and then Highway 1.

Above: Marina del Rey - a man-made harbor capable of accommodating up to 7,000 boats.

Left: A 1950s poster advertising a show by 'surf guitarist' Dick Dale on the Balboa peninsula.

Left: A miniature replica of the gateway to Santa Monica's famous pier.

Below: This local college, founded in 1929, has many famous alumni.

Above: Laguna Beach, to the south of Los Angeles, seen from just off Laguna Avenue.

Below: The ocean itself helps to safeguard the privacy of Malibu's beachfront residents: anyone coming too close to their properties (especially at high tide) is likely to get wet feet!

After leaving Ventura (see pages 144–145), we drive south to Oxnard on Highway 101. Here, Highway 1 splits away to the right, heading first down Oxnard Boulevard and then along Pidduck Road, en route for the Pacific shore. Having reached the ocean,

Both photographs below: Grand mansions like the ones pictured here can be seen in some profusion beside and (especially) above the Pacific Coast Highway as it passes though Malibu en route for Santa Monica.

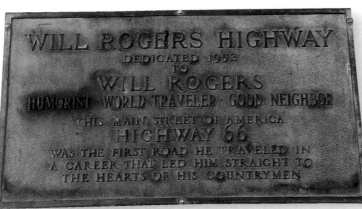

Above: This plaque, in Palisades Park, celebrates the dedication of Route 66 (which ends close by) to one of Oklahoma's most famous sons, performer and columnist Will Rogers.

we continue south past the Leo Carrillo State Beach, named for the actor who appeared opposite Duncan Renaldo in the classic *Cisco Kid* 1950s TV series. The beach lies close to the Los Angeles county line, and about 15 miles further on, we approach the exclusive enclave of Malibu—one of the most sought-after locations on this entire coastline.

The land around Malibu, originally a ranch property, was purchased in 1891 by Frederick Hastings Rindge (author of the popular memoir *Happy Days in Southern California*—see pages 166–167), and, until the late 1920s, his family successfully fought off plans for highway and railroad developments there.

These legal battles were extended and costly, and eventually, Rindge's widow was forced to restore her finances by leasing (and then selling) parts of her estate for residential use by rich movie actors and executives. The Malibu neighborhood—and especially its famous beachfront—was soon colonized by Hollywood "names," and, in later years, it has also attracted top sportsmen, rock musicians, and other members of the LA aristocracy.

commemorative artworks, including a plaque to humorist Will Rogers, who was closely associated with Route 66 – the great Chicago–Los Angeles highway that terminates at the junction of Ocean and Santa Monica Boulevard.

Below Another fine home – with a strongly patriotic garage door – overlooking Santa Monica Bay.

> ❝ **In the early days of radio, comedians knew they could milk a sure-fire laugh with a joke about the Los Angeles city limits…The city is a monument to urban sprawl.** ❞
>
> *Bill Harris, Pacific Coast Highway –*
> *A Photographic Journey, 1991*

Right The junction of Ocean Avenue (with Palisades Park to its left) and Santa Monica Boulevard is the official terminus of Route 66.

Highway 1 passes the back doors of Malibu's bayside mansions, and stretches on towards the surfers' paradise of Topanga Beach. Beyond it are Pacific Palisades and Santa Monica, where the cool green strip of Palisades Park runs above and to the left of the road. Take the California Incline exit up onto Ocean Avenue for a closer look at the Park, which contains a number of interesting statues and

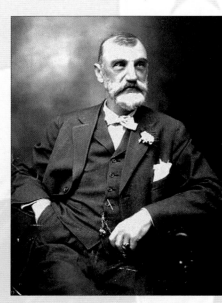

Below: New Jersey-born entrepreneur Abbot Kinney, whose "Venice of America" opened, on the site of what is now Venice Beach, in 1905.

Above: Looking down the length of Santa Monica Pier from near its 'Yacht Harbor' entrance gateway (which was pictured on page 151). The pier area covers some nine acres.

Walk along Ocean Avenue to Colorado Avenue; to the right is the entrance to Santa Monica's famous Pier, the oldest part of which (the Municipal Pier) dates from 1909. Its early success caught the attention of Charles Looff (1852–1918), a German émigré who had designed and constructed carousels for New York's Coney Island resort, and had gone on to create similar amusements on both the East and West Coasts. In 1916, he built a second pier (adjacent to the existing one) at Santa Monica; it offered a range of attractions, including a roller-coaster and carousel, that had locals and tourists flocking to it in their thousands.

The piers flourished throughout the next few decades, but later fell into a gradual decline, accelerated by the launch of Disneyland in 1955. By 1973 the City authorities had determined to demolish them; however, a vigorous conservation campaign (backed by Robert Redford and Paul Newman, whose Oscar-winning movie *The Sting*, released that year, used the pier site as a location) succeeded in reversing this decision, and precipitated a program of much-needed repair and refurbishment. This brought back the visitors, and the pier's appeal received a further boost in 1996, with the opening of its new "Pacific Park" funfair.

Our next Los Angeles destination, Venice Beach, lies just beyond Santa Monica; to reach it, drive southeast on Ocean Avenue, and then continue on Neilson Way and Pacific Avenue. The pedestrian thoroughfare of Ocean Front Walk runs parallel to the beach from near Ozone, which intersects with Pacific. A stroll from here to the junction with Washington Street, just over two miles away, takes us past a succession of stores and street vendors selling gaudy knick-knacks; to the right are palm trees, stretches of grass, pathways populated by roller-skaters and skateboarders, and, beyond them, the sand and the sea. The area has its own distinctive charm, but bears little resemblance to the original Venice Beach, which was developed by tobacco magnate Abbot Kinney (1850–1920) in the 1900s, and featured a pier, amusement arcades, and a network of canals.

Above: Bikes are well provided for at Venice Beach, with numerous safe, clearly marked riding tracks.

Above left: Highway 1 (Palisades Beach Road) runs though Santa Monica almost at sea level north of the Pier; Palisades Park and Ocean Avenue lie above it.

Left and center inset: Venice Beach's sidewalk and waterfront is a popular place for sports and leisure activities.

Far left: The Venice Beach Boardwalk offers an amazing variety of shops and stalls.

153

LA, Movies, Music & Media

Below, left and right: The Grateful Dead and Frank Sinatra - two of the many star names signed to LA record labels.

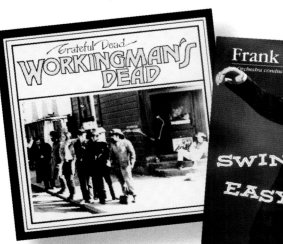

In 1911, the first Hollywood film studio, Nestor, opened its doors on Sunset Boulevard, and within little more than a decade, many of the biggest names in movie production, including Universal, United Artists, and Warner Brothers, had established themselves in Los Angeles. The scale and speed of their success elevated the motion picture industry from its former, lowly status—early movies had been derisively named "the flickers" by some actors and critics—into what journalist Alistair Cooke described as "the most flourishing factory of popular mythology since the Greeks." It also made LA a magnet for creative talent, laying the foundations for the city's future importance as a center for other mass media.

Los Angeles' music scene grew rapidly from the 1940s onwards, boosted by a combination of homegrown talent, migrants from the East, and

Above and right: Former Santa Monica College students include Dustin Hoffman. Right: Pacific Palisades High School – attended by actor Jeff Bridges.

performers who stayed in Southern California after completing their War service there. Local record labels flourished: Capitol signed Frank Sinatra in 1953, and the 1960s saw the launch of A & M, co-owned by trumpeter Herb Alpert. But the biggest newly-emerging player in the LA music industry was Warner Brothers, which, from the mid-60s on, assembled a matchless roster of rock artists—many of whom had a distinctively "Californian" sound that influenced pop for decades. Among them were The Grateful Dead (Warners' first rock signing), Fleetwood Mac—and acts such as The Eagles, Jackson Browne, and Guns N' Roses, who recorded for Asylum and Geffen, the Warner-affiliated labels run by entrepreneur David Geffen.

Geffen has subsequently branched out into movies, most recently as co-founder of DreamWorks; while Warner itself is now part of the massive conglomerate AOL Time Warner, and other deals and mergers have further blurred the once clear distinctions between LA's film, record, TV and "new media" companies. But the city and its surrounding area seems unlikely ever to lose its preeminent position as America's cultural "nerve center." According to Joel Kotkin and Paul Grabowicz's *California Inc.*, 90% of all the world's recorded entertainment originated there in 1980; the figure has undoubtedly risen since then.

Above: Warner Bros.' West Hollywood premises, nicknamed 'The Lot.'
Top: The Capitol Records Building at 1750 Vine Street, Hollywood.

Bottom photograph: Marina del Rey, and the crescent-shaped sand of Marina Beach, photographed from the top of the Marriott Hotel on Admiralty Way.

Below: Manhattan Beach and its distinctively turreted pier, seen from Ocean Drive.

After visiting Venice Beach, drive away from the shore up Washington Street. Immediately to the right of the road here is Marina del Rey, a complex of hotels, restaurants, stores, apartments and office blocks surrounding a 7-basin, man-made harbor that provides docking space for over 6,000 small boats.

Its completion in 1965 was the realization of plans dating back to the 1880s, when property developer M.C. Wicks first proposed turning the marshland around Playa del Rey (the King's Beach) into a commercial shipping terminal. Wicks' ideas proved impractical and led him to financial ruin, and later port projects also came to

nothing. However, by the 1940s, support was growing for the construction of a pleasure boat harbor here, and building work (which also involved the provision of an offshore breakwater to protect the Marina from wave damage) finally commenced in 1957. Today, the Marina is a flourishing center for leisure and business, and an agreeable place for a meal or a drink. Enter it from Washington Street by turning right onto Via Marina, and then bearing left onto Admiralty Way, which runs around the harbor basins. Beyond Basin H is a junction with Fiji Way: turn right here for the popular Fisherman's Village dining and shopping area, or left to head for Highway 1 (Lincoln Boulevard) and continue south.

Right: Another view of Marina del Rey. Nearby buildings include offices and apartments as well as hotels and restaurants.

We spend little time on Lincoln, exiting from it onto West Jefferson Boulevard, and then taking Culver Boulevard to Vista del Mar, which skirts the perimeter of LA International Airport and passes Dockweiler State Beach as it runs parallel to the shore. Vista del Mar becomes Highland Avenue before intersecting with Manhattan Beach Boulevard; turn right at the junction and drive towards the ocean to see this popular surfing beach and its famous concrete pier—built in 1920, and recently made a State Historic Landmark. The city of Manhattan Beach began as a small group of vacation homes, erected here in the early 1900s and named by its New York-born developer, John Merrill; it was incorporated in 1912, and its population now numbers some 34,000.

Above: A seemingly endless sweep of sand extends north from Manhattan Beach. This picture was taken from the pier.

Dennis Wilson

Manhattan Beach was famously mentioned in The Beach Boys' classic 1963 single Surfin' USA, and the band's songs epitomized the fun-loving, wave-chasing spirit of '60s Californian youth. However, only one of the three Wilson brothers at The Beach Boys' core was actually a surfer: drummer and vocalist Dennis, who spent much of his teenage leisure time on Manhattan Beach (just southwest of the family home in Hawthorne), and first suggested that the group should sing about the sport. Dennis retained his love for the ocean throughout his often-troubled later career—during which he suffered from alcoholism and drug addiction, and sustained a hand injury that led to a lengthy break from onstage work. By the early 1980s, though, he was managing to combine his Beach Boys commitments with solo recording projects—but tragedy struck on December 28 1983, when he drowned at Marina del Rey after taking a drunken dive into the water near his boat, the Harmony. He was 39 years old.

Below: Shelly Manne (1920-1984) – one of the top jazzmen who appeared at Hermosa Beach's Lighthouse Café.

Below: Redondo Beach and its famous pier, which has recently benefited from a million-dollar refurbishment program.

The easiest route south from Manhattan Beach is via Highway 1 (Sepulveda Boulevard); to reach it, drive east (away from the ocean) along Manhattan Beach Boulevard, which intersects with the main road after a few blocks. Then continue down Sepulveda for about two miles, and turn right onto Pier Avenue for Hermosa Beach.

Like Manhattan and Redondo Beaches, Hermosa was once part of the 22,000-acre Rancho Sausal Redondo (literally, "the circular ranch with willow trees"), a Mexican land grant which was later broken up into separate holdings. In the early 1900s, part of the old rancho, including Hermosa, was acquired by entrepreneurs Moses Sherman and Eli Clark, who constructed a railroad linking it with central Los Angeles. Incorporated in 1907, Hermosa Beach soon became a favorite spot for vacationers. Among its regular summer visitors was William Jennings Bryan (1860–1925), the lawyer and Democratic congressman

now best remembered for his involvement in the 1925 prosecution of John Scopes for teaching the principles of Darwinian evolution in Tennessee.

Bryan would doubtless have disapproved of the goings-on at Hermosa Beach's most celebrated music venue, the Lighthouse Café on Pier Avenue. Here, in the late 40s and 50s, some of Southern California's leading musicians (such as saxophonist Gerry Mulligan, drummer Shelly Manne, and bassist Howard Rumsey) laid the foundations for modern West Coast jazz. The Lighthouse remains a thriving nightspot, though its musical policy now embraces a wider range of pop and rock styles.

Redondo Beach, a little to the south (take Highway 1 to the Torrance Boulevard junction, then drive west towards its waterfront), has been a busy

Above and above inset: Pier Avenue, Hermosa Beach's main entertainment and leisure hotspot. At No. 30 is the Lighthouse Café music venue (see inset photo), almost adjacent to which is the Surf City Hostel (see far right photo), with its strikingly decorated front door.

harbor, and a center for business and leisure, since the 1890s. However, its greatest claim to fame is as the place where surfing was first introduced to California by George Freeth (1883–1919—no relation to the author), a Hawaiian-Irishman hired by Redondo's principal landowner, Henry E. Huntington, in 1907 to attract visitors and serve as a municipal lifeguard. Freeth's aquatic skills earned him the sobriquet "the man who could walk on water;" a memorial to him stands on the city's pier.

Lower right: Looking back along the coast from Palos Verdes Drive West and Paseo del Mar.

Below: The tower of the Wayfarers' Chapel was completed a few years after the rest of the building, in 1954.

From Torrance Boulevard in Redondo Beach, head south on Prospect Avenue, which connects with Palos Verdes Boulevard. A right turn now brings us to Palos Verdes Drive—the road that leads around the Palos Verdes ("green branches") peninsula towards San Pedro. This former ranch land was purchased by a syndicate led by East Coast banker Frank A. Vanderlip in 1913, and transformed, during the following decade, into an elegant, exclusive residential area by Frederick Law Olmsted Jr., whose father, Frederick Sr., had created New York's Central Park in the 1860s and 70s. Strict regulations prohibit the erection of billboards or other visual intrusions here, and limits on new building ensure that the surrounding landscape retains its peaceful spaciousness—which is enhanced by the superb coastal views from its bluffs and beaches.

The peninsula's most striking and original building is the Wayfarers' Chapel on the southern section of Palos Verdes Drive, just beyond Point Vicente. Designed for the Swedenborgian Church by Lloyd Wright (1890–1978—the son of architect Frank Lloyd Wright), the Chapel dates from 1951; its glass roof and walls are intended to promote what Wright described as a sense of "outer as well as

inner space" among visitors and worshippers. The other principal materials used in its construction are redwood and local stone, and Wright was also responsible for the layout of the trees and plants that encircle the site. The 50-foot tower, topped by a gold leaf cross, was completed in 1954.

On leaving the Chapel, continue along Palos Verdes Drive and West 25th Street, before turning right onto Western Avenue and driving down to explore the Royal Palms County Beach. From there, take Paseo del Mar into San Pedro, and turn north

Above: The view northwest from Angel's Gate Park in San Pedro, near the site of the Korean Friendship Bell.
Left: The interior of Lloyd Wright's Wayfarers' Chapel, 5755 South Rancho Palos Verdes Drive. Wright conceived the building as "a natural sanctuary."
Center: The Korean Friendship Bell and its surrounding pagoda cost over half a million dollars to erect. As well as celebrating the American Bicentennial, they also commemorate those who died in the Korean War.

(left) onto Gaffey Street. At Gaffey and 37th lies Angel's Gate Park: here, overlooking the ocean, stands the 17-ton Korean Friendship Bell, a present to the American people from the Republic of Korea to mark the Bicentennial Jubilee in 1976. The huge bell carries a range of delicate decorative carvings, including four pairs of goddess figures symbolizing Freedom, Independence, Peace and Prosperity.

161

The *Queen Mary*

Below and bottom left: The Queen Mary *in her oceangoing days – and moored in Long Beach, with a Soviet submarine positioned (rather incongrously) alongside.*

The 81,000-ton *Queen Mary* ocean liner has been moored at Long Beach for over three decades, and is the area's leading tourist attraction. She is easily reached from San Pedro by turning onto Highway 47 from North Gaffey Street, driving across the Vincent Thomas Bridge, and heading along West Ocean Boulevard to the Pico Avenue exit. From here, take South Pico Avenue, and follow the signs for the *Queen Mary*, which is located at Pier J.

With the coming of World War II, the *Queen Mary* and her larger sister ship, the *Queen Elizabeth* (launched in 1938, but not used for civilian transportation until 1946), were converted into troop carriers. The "two Queens" covered hundreds

The vessel has a remarkable history. Built for the Cunard Line, she was named in honor of the wife of Britain's King George V; the King and Queen presided over her launch in 1934, and her maiden voyage from Southampton to New York City took place two years later. She was the fastest and the most luxurious ship of her class and period, taking little more than four days to complete a transatlantic crossing, and offering her 2,000 passengers an unrivalled range of amenities—including swimming pools, Turkish baths, cinemas, childrens' playrooms, and numerous bars and restaurants. There was even a synagogue and Kosher kitchen onboard.

of thousands of sea miles during the years of conflict, and Sir Winston Churchill later commented that "without their aid the day of final victory [would] unquestionably have been postponed." They resumed regular commercial Atlantic crossings in 1947; but the subsequent growth of long-haul air travel gradually reduced their passenger numbers and profitability, and in the mid-60s Cunard sold off both ships. *Queen Mary* was acquired by the City of Long Beach after completing her final voyage in December 1967; she is currently managed by a non-profitmaking foundation which operates her as a hotel and restaurant, and offers regular tours of her carefully preserved decks and interiors. (Visitors can also admire the Russian 'Scorpion' submarine moored alongside her.) Her less fortunate sister was destroyed by fire in Hong Kong Harbor in 1972.

Below RMS Queen Mary in her permanent berth at 1126 Queens Highway, Long Beach. Built in the Scottish shipyards at Clydebank, and described at the time of her launch by King George V of Great Britain as "the stateliest ship afloat", the historic ocean liner is this area's main tourist attraction.

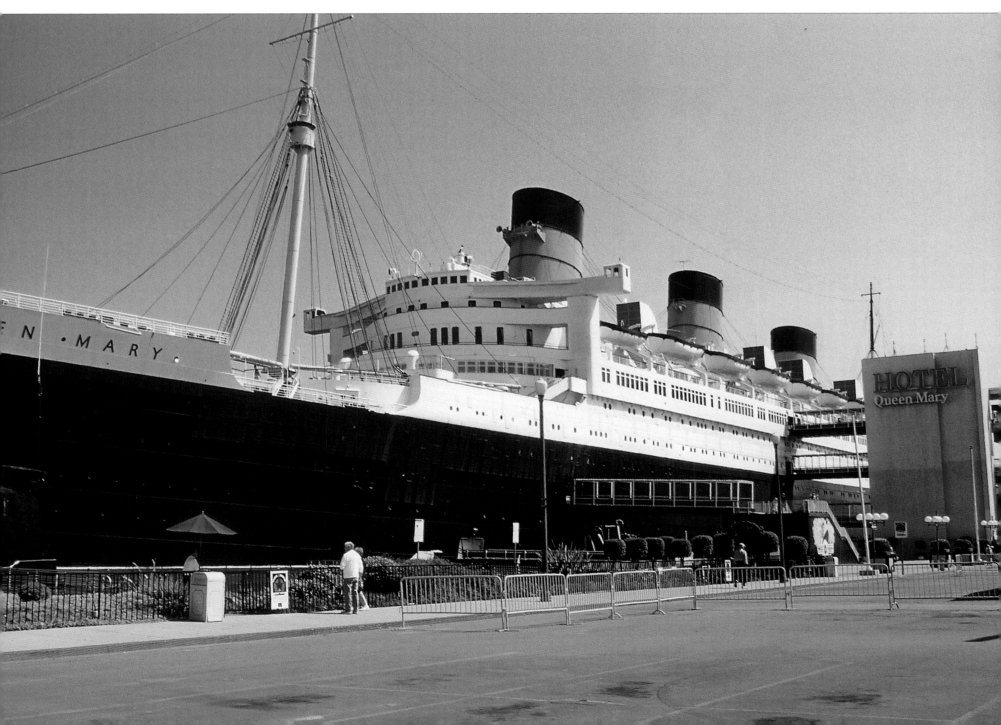

CALIFORNIA REPUBLIC
CALIFORNIA

Oxnard | 1886 | Santa Monica | 1900 | Marina del Rey | 1910 | Hermosa Beach
1850 | Malibu | 1898 | Venice Beach | 1902 | Manhattan Beach | 1912

Below: The Long Beach skyline and waterfront. Initially named Willmore (for its original developer), the city celebrated its centenary in 1988.

Right and bottom: Huntington Pier, near Pacific Coast Highway and Main in Huntington Beach, is the longest concrete municipal pier in California.

It was once possible to combine a visit to the *Queen Mary* with a look at Howard Hughes' "Spruce Goose" flying boat, displayed in the huge geodesic dome next to the liner. (The 8-engine, 150-ton airplane made its one and only flight, over Long Beach harbor, in November 1947.) However, in 1992, the Goose was moved to McMinnville, Oregon, and the dome, now used by Warner Brothers as a movie soundstage, is no longer open to the public. The only other significant site near the *Queen Mary* is the Queen's Marketplace "English-style village," containing shops, cafés and restaurants.

To see some more of Long Beach, cross Queensway Bridge, which leads towards the Shoreline Village and Marina, both dating from 1982. Also close by is the largest recent development in this area, the Aquarium of the Pacific, opened in 1998 and occupying some 120,000 square feet. Such new sites, though attractive and profitable, have inevitably encroached on Long Beach's greatest natural asset: in 2000, a local conservationist, Ann Cantrell, commented that "[during] my lifetime, [the city] has lost 5 miles of beach and now only 6 miles are left of the original 11 miles of beach coastline. I would like to die in Long Beach, NOT Short Beach!"

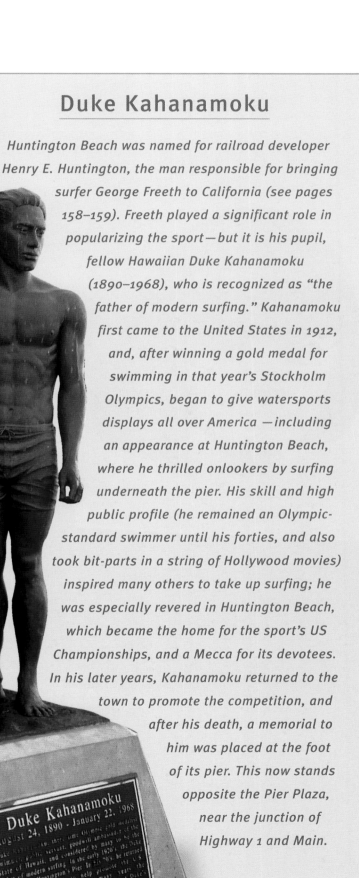

Duke Kahanamoku

Huntington Beach was named for railroad developer Henry E. Huntington, the man responsible for bringing surfer George Freeth to California (see pages 158–159). Freeth played a significant role in popularizing the sport—but it is his pupil, fellow Hawaiian Duke Kahanamoku (1890–1968), who is recognized as "the father of modern surfing." Kahanamoku first came to the United States in 1912, and, after winning a gold medal for swimming in that year's Stockholm Olympics, began to give watersports displays all over America —including an appearance at Huntington Beach, where he thrilled onlookers by surfing underneath the pier. His skill and high public profile (he remained an Olympic-standard swimmer until his forties, and also took bit-parts in a string of Hollywood movies) inspired many others to take up surfing; he was especially revered in Huntington Beach, which became the home for the sport's US Championships, and a Mecca for its devotees. In his later years, Kahanamoku returned to the town to promote the competition, and after his death, a memorial to him was placed at the foot of its pier. This now stands opposite the Pier Plaza, near the junction of Highway 1 and Main.

Fortunately, there are still excellent, uninterrupted views across San Pedro Bay as we turn right along Shoreline Drive and continue south on East Ocean Boulevard. Near Belmont Shore, we move briefly inland on 2nd Street before rejoining Highway 1 and crossing into Orange County. Between Seal and Sunset Beaches, the marshy expanse of a wildlife reserve opens out to our left; beyond here, the coast stretches away southeast to Huntington Beach, whose 1,856-foot concrete pier (a modern reconstruction of the one completed in 1914 and extended in 1930) is visible from far away. The city, named in 1904 and incorporated five years later, was formerly a booming oil town; but since the last substantial strike in the early 1950s, it has become more famous as a center for tourism and—thanks to its eight miles of sandy shoreline—surfing.

Right, bottom left and right: Laguna – named 'Canada de las Lagunas' (Canyon of the Lakes) by its first Spanish settlers.
Below: This region has had its share of tragedy: actress Natalie Wood drowned off Catalina Island in 1981.

South of Huntington Beach lies Newport Beach—a quiet backwater before its late nineteenth century transformation into a bustling seafreight terminus, with the opening of a shipping wharf on the site of the present pier by local businessmen Robert and James McFadden. The provision of a rail link to the wharf in 1905 gave a further boost to the surrounding region's fortunes, and the following year, Newport Beach was incorporated as a city; the nearby waterfront communities of Balboa and Corona del Mar also fall within its boundaries. Before long, Newport was attracting wealthy vacationers and settlers from Los Angeles and beyond, and it remains a favored spot for the super-rich. However, it also has a wider appeal— and a special place in the hearts of many popular music fans as the source of the quintessentially Californian "surf guitar" sound.

> 66 'Do you like Southern California?'
> 'Well,' said the Californian, 'I do love the Sunset-land.
> There is much to enjoy. Nature is at its best; in that new
> wonderland is a glorious serenity, and yet human energy
> is not lost as in most semi-tropical countries.
> It is a blending of the temperate zone with the tropic.
> A wonderful ocean current coming across the sea
> from Japan is a benediction to that coast country.
> Ah! Southern California is peculiar to itself!' 99

Frederick Hastings Rindge (1857-1905), Happy Days in Southern California *(1898)*

Above: Balboa Pavilion, at Main and Balboa Boulevard. This historic building, now a restaurant, is the departure point for the Catalina Island boat service.

This was developed by surfer-turned-musician Dick Dale, whose appearances at the Rendezvous Ballroom on the Balboa Peninsula from the mid-1950s onwards showcased a distinctive, high-volume guitar sound (created with instruments and amplifiers designed by fellow Orange County resident Leo Fender), and a gift for memorable riffs and melodies that attracted thousands of screaming fans. Dale retains a devoted cult following; but sadly, the Rendezvous was destroyed by fire in 1966. However, a rival venue, the Pavilion, survives intact at 400 Main Street; to get there, head right from Highway 1 along Balboa Boulevard (passing the turn-off for Newport Pier en route). A former bath house dating from 1905, the Pavilion is still in regular use for dining and dancing, and also serves as a booking office for boat trips around the coast and to Catalina Island, about 20 miles offshore.

After exploring the Peninsula, return to Highway 1, and continue, past Corona Del Mar State Beach and Emerald Bay, towards the elegant city of Laguna Beach, once a small village made up of homesteaders and a few artists, but now boasting a population of some 24,000. It merges almost seamlessly into South Laguna, a more recently developed area that was annexed by its larger neighbor in 1989.

167

South to Tijuana

Highway 1, our main coastal thoroughfare for hundreds of miles, ends just beyond South Laguna, at Dana Point; from here, we take a short detour north on I-5 to the Mission San Juan Capistrano before continuing (using both the freeway and S21, the old shoreline road) towards San Diego via San Clemente, Oceanside and Carlsbad. Our long journey concludes with a trip across the Mexican border – the original destination of US Highway 101 when it was commissioned in 1926 – to Tijuana.

Above: San Diego's elegant parks and gardens are a peaceful haven for its residents and visitors.

CALIFORNIA REPUBLIC

CALIFORNIA

| South Laguna | 1971 | Mission San Juan Capistrano | 1982 | Oceanside | 2008 | Leucadia |
| 1968 | Dana Point | 1975 | San Clemente | 2004 | Carlsbad | 2017 |

South to Tijuana

Above: Tijuana's El Torrito bar and disco caters mainly for the tourist trade.

Below: Some Like It Hot *(1959) was shot at the Hotel del Coronado.*

San Diego, originally called San Miguel by Juan Rodríguez Cabrillo in 1542 (see pages 148–149), owes its present name to Sebastián Vizcaíno, the merchant-turned-explorer who sailed into the harbor where the city now stands on November 10, 1602—two days before the feast of Saint Didacus (Diego) of Alcalá, for whom Vizcaíno's own ship had already been christened. His party took a brief trip ashore, noting what Father Antonio de la Ascensión, a priest attached to the expedition, described as "the fertility and good character" of the surrounding land. The sharp-eyed padre also observed the presence of pyrites (sparkling yellow fragments of iron sulphide) in the soil and rocks, believing them to be a sure indication of gold deposits in the mountains to the east—a hope that later proved groundless, though this did little to detract from the appeal of the region to subsequent settlers.

San Diego itself began to take shape in the 1820s, briefly becoming the center of Californian political life when the province's governor from 1825 to 1831, José María Echeandía, chose to base himself there; the climate of the nominal capital, Monterey, was said to aggravate his chronic rheumatism. By the end of Mexican rule, the Old Town area south of the Presidio (see pages 180–183) was well established, and in 1850, development of the "New Town" nearer the harbor (now the Gaslamp Quarter) was started by a group of entrepreneurs led by William Heath Davis (1822–1909). Their plans were soon thwarted by financial difficulties, but the New Town scheme was taken up in 1867 by Alonzo Erastus Horton (1813–1909), who made (and later lost) a fortune from land and building deals in what was soon to be the heart of San Diego, and is often referred to as the city's founding father.

Below: A sign above the entrance to a shopping mall in downtown Tijuana.

Below: Neimans Restaurant in Carlsbad.

Above: The beach and pier at San Clemente.

CALIFORNIA REPUBLIC

During the 1880s, the construction of coastal railroad links to San Diego and other Californian destinations led to the emergence of towns such as Oceanside and Carlsbad; and in 1906, work began on a line to link San Diego with Yuma, Arizona, the terminus of the Southern Pacific service to Los Angeles and San Francisco. This was finished in 1919—by which time, a paved coastal highway was already in place from the Mexican border to LA, completing a comprehensive network of transportation for a part of America that had once been considered remote and isolated. With improved access came new residents and vacationers eager to enjoy the temperate weather—as well as the first sprinkling of Hollywood stars and other millionaire visitors who would later colonize large stretches of this most elegant and well-groomed of shorelines.

Above: San Diego's Hotel del Coronado became a State Historical Landmark in 1970.

Below: Tijuana offers a taste of Mexico for visitors from the US.

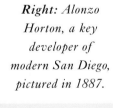

Right: Alonzo Horton, a key developer of modern San Diego, pictured in 1887.

Right: Painted and stained glass items for sale on Tijuana's main drag, Avenida Revolución.

171

San Juan Capistrano

These pages: The exquisite gardens and grounds of the Mission San Juan Capistrano – and the interior of the 'Serra Chapel.'

The Mission San Juan Capistrano is located in the little town that shares its name, near the intersection of the Ortega Highway and Camino Capistrano. To reach it, take I-5 north from its junction with Highway 1 beyond Dana Point; alternatively, turn off 1 onto Del Obispo Street (just before crossing the San Juan Creek at the southern edge of Dana Point), follow the road to its junction with Camino Capistrano, and head left.

The founder of what came to be called "the Jewel of the Missions" was Father Fermín Lasuén, who dedicated the ground on which it stands in 1775, but was forced to abandon building work after being summoned to San Diego, which was under threat from hostile natives (see pages 182–183). The following year, San Juan Capistrano was re-established by Junípero Serra, Father-President of the Missions. He supervised the construction of various now-vanished adobe dwellings and storerooms, but his most important creation, the "Serra Chapel," is still in regular use. Completed in 1777, it is the only surviving church where Serra is known to have celebrated Mass.

In the 1790s, plans were drawn up for a larger place of worship to accommodate San Juan Capistrano's growing numbers of neophytes, soldiers and clergy. The new "Great Stone Church," an imposing edifice made from a combination of locally quarried sandstone and red brick, took almost a decade to complete. However, in 1812, just

six years after its dedication, it was severely damaged in an earthquake that occurred during a service, claiming the lives of many of the congregation. The church was never rebuilt, and its ruined walls and arches are a poignant reminder of the disaster.

In contrast, several other parts of the Mission, which suffered from looting and other depredations after it was secularized in 1833, have now been restored to their former glory, enabling visitors to appreciate their rich historical and religious significance. The site's other attractions include its beautiful gardens, as well as the presence, in season, of the famous Capistrano swallows (immortalized in Leon Rene's classic song) which return there to nest every March.

> **The country stretched out for miles as far as the eye could reach, on a level, table surface; and the only habitation in sight was the small white mission of San Juan Capistrano, with a few Indian huts about it, standing in a small hollow, about a mile from where we were.**
>
> *Richard Henry Dana, Jr.,* Two Years Before The Mast, *1840*

173

Above and top: Richard Nixon,
a longtime resident of San Clemente,
standing outside the 'Western White
House' (Casa Pacifica); and Nixon
and his wife Pat, pictured in the 1960s
relaxing on the town's beach.

From the Mission, drive south on Camino Capistrano for a couple of miles, and then bear right onto Doheny Park Road, which leads to Doheny State Beach. Turn left here, and follow the road along the shore for about three miles before taking El Camino Real into San Clemente.

This pretty, Spanish-style town was the brainchild of Ole Hanson (1874–1940), a native of Wisconsin who had qualified as a lawyer, worked as a traveling salesman and insurance broker, and served as mayor of Seattle before moving to Los Angeles and embarking on a successful series of real estate deals. He used the proceeds from these to fund the creation of San Clemente on a stretch of undeveloped coast land which he had earmarked as an ideal site for a "Spanish Village" many years earlier, after catching sight of it from a train. Hanson's plans were announced to the press in November 1925; and on December 6 that year, he began selling building lots for the new town from a tent pitched in the mud on what is now its Avenida Del Mar. Demand exceeded all expectations: Hanson's first day's sales totaled over $125,000, and by the end of 1926, plots worth more than $4 million had been purchased.

Residents were contractually obliged to build their houses and business premises in "the Spanish style" and to have them approved by an 'architectural board', and Hanson himself was responsible for commissioning San Clemente's most outstanding property: the Spanish-Colonial "Casa Romantica," which was his home from 1928 until 1932. Located on Avenida Granada (which connects with El Camino Real and runs down towards the sea), it is now owned by the city authorities, and has recently been reopened to the public after undergoing extensive renovation. Its architect, Carl Lindbom, also designed another famous local residence, "La Casa Pacifica"—better known as the "Western White House," former home of Richard Nixon. Appropriately, the road leading towards it has been named Avenida Del Presidente; however, the mansion itself is closed to visitors, though it can be glimpsed from nearby San Clemente State Beach.

Above: The San Clemente Municipal Pier, seen at sunset. It was designed and built by Ole Hanson as part of the original town he created here.

Left: An archive picture of Casa Romantica, courtesy of the Heritage of San Clemente Foundation. (The building itself was under renovation at the time of writing.)

Above: A aerial postcard view of Casa Pacifica – with an inset shot of its most famous occupant.

Nixon and the 'Western White House'

Richard Milhous Nixon (1913–1994) was born in the Southern Californian town of Yorba Linda, and retained a lifelong love for the region's countryside and coastline. In 1969, the year in which he was sworn in as 37th President of the United States, he purchased a house and grounds overlooking the ocean at San Clemente; the estate had formerly been the property of Hamilton H. Cotton, one of Ole Hanson's principal business partners (see opposite). Nixon named it "Casa Pacifica," and used it both as a family retreat and a place for presidential meetings and photo opportunities. Distinguished guests at the "Western White House" included South Vietnamese President Nguyen Van Thieu, Soviet Premier Leonid Brezhnev, and Japanese Prime Minister Eisaku Sato—and during President Nixon's frequent periods in residence there, the streets of San Clemente were transformed by an influx of aides, officials and security staff. Tranquility was restored after his resignation in 1974, although he and his wife continued to live in Casa Pacifica until 1980.

Top: 'Alt Karlsbad' on Carlsbad Boulevard. The statue to the right depicts Captain John Frazier, who discovered the local water's properties in 1882. Above: Carlsbad's train station, a few blocks to the east.

the thirteenth-century French saint, monarch and hero of the Crusades. The largest of California's twenty-one missions, most of its buildings were designed by Lasuén's successor, Father Antonio Peyri, and built by local Indian labor. To reach it, take Highway 76 east from its junction with the interstate at the northern edge of Oceanside; the Mission lies about 4 miles away, near the exit for Rancho del Oro Drive.

Returning to I-5, we continue south to Carlsbad, where we leave the freeway at the Carlsbad Village Drive exit, head past the old Santa Fe depot (dating from 1907, and now a tourist information center), and turn right onto Carlsbad Boulevard (S21) to visit the site of the well whose mineral water led to

On the south side of San Clemente, join I-5 from El Camino Real, and stay on the freeway as it crosses into San Diego County and runs close to the perimeter of Camp Pendleton—a vast Marine Corps base, established in 1942 and occupying approximately 125,000 acres of former rancho land. To our right, near the railroad tracks, is Old Highway 101 (renamed S21 farther south), which offers a more leisurely drive than I-5, and gives easier access to the towns and beaches on our route —although, for speed and convenience, many travelers will probably prefer to use the Interstate as their main thoroughfare for the rest of our journey.

Camp Pendleton stretches on for some 17 miles before we reach the outskirts of Oceanside: leave I-5 here to explore the city, which owes much of its postwar expansion and prosperity to close links with its massive military neighbor. The other major place of interest in this area is the Mission San Luis Rey de Francia, set up in 1798 and named by its founder, Father Fermín Lasuén, for Louis IX,

the founding of a thriving spa here in the 1880s. After decades of disuse, it has recently been reactivated, providing a source for bottled water and also supplying the new Carlsbad Mineral Water Spa, opened in 1997 and located in the adjacent Alt Karlsbad building.

Right: The first of the three flagpoles outside the Mission flies the Stars and Stripes and the Californian State flag. The other two flags on display there are those of Spain and Mexico.

Below: Mission San Luis Rey de Francia, near Oceanside. Its church was completed in 1815, and substantially restored during the early years of the twentieth century.

Both below: Encinitas' Quail Botanical Gardens displays and preserves many rare plant species.

We remain on S21 (Carlsbad Boulevard) for the next few miles, as the old coast road passes the Carlsbad and South Carlsbad State Beaches, and crosses the mouth of the Batiquitos Lagoon before entering Leucadia. The highway here is lined with eucalyptus trees, planted, like the cypresses that also grace this area, by the town's late nineteenth century developers—hard-headed businessmen with a seemingly soft spot for Classical literature and mythology, who called their new settlement by the Greek term for "a sheltered place," named many of its streets after Hellenic and Roman deities (Neptune, Hygeia, Vulcan, Eolus), and described available housing land as "villa lots" on early prospectuses. Today, Leucadia is part of the adjacent city of Encinitas, which is also home to the famous Quail Botanical Gardens—set up in 1943 to display the private plant collection of Charles and Ruth Larabee, and run since 1961 by a non-profitmaking foundation dedicated to cultivating and conserving flora from throughout the world. To visit the Gardens, take Encinitas Boulevard from S21 (Vulcan Avenue), continue past the junction with I-5 to the intersection with Quail Gardens Drive, and turn left.

Travelers can now choose either to return to S21 for a peaceful drive beside the ocean via Cardiff-by-the-Sea and Solana Beach, or to take a swifter route south on I-5. Both roads lead towards Del Mar (about 7 miles away—the freeway skirts its eastern

Above and right: The Del Mar Fairgrounds offer a range of facilities – including the 'Surfside Raceplace', which provides satellite coverage of horseracing from other tracks.

edge), and the famous Fairgrounds on Jimmy Durante Boulevard. Originally a county fair site, built as part of an employment-providing Works Progress Administration scheme in 1936, the Fairgrounds soon became a successful horseracing venue, attracting the support and patronage of Hollywood stars like Durante and Bing Crosby, and have subsequently expanded into a major center for a variety of sporting events, shows and conferences. The nearby town, founded as a tent city in the 1880s, is now an affluent residential community.

Our final port of call on this stretch of coast is La Jolla—an elegant oceanside settlement whose former residents include mystery writer Raymond Chandler (1888–1959), and Theodor Seuss Geisel (1904–1991), better known as Dr. Seuss, creator of *The Cat In The Hat*. Chandler's barbed description of the area as "a nice place for old people and their parents" now seems somewhat wide of the mark; since his day, its energy levels

Above: The Heritage Park in San Diego's Old Town.
Left: La Jolla is one of this region's top beach resorts.

have been boosted by the presence of a major college campus just to the north (The University of California, San Diego), and there is certainly no shortage of youth or liveliness on the town's busy beaches and streets. La Jolla lies a little west of I-5: to get there, take the Ardath Road exit and then follow Torrey Pines Road (which also forms part of the pre-interstate coastal route) towards the shore.

A few miles to the south, use of the freeways becomes unavoidable as we enter San Diego. Thankfully, though, the city's congestion levels are lower than those in Los Angeles, and most destinations are clearly signposted—including the Presidio and Old Town sites that are first on our itinerary. Immediately after crossing the San Diego River Floodway on I-5, we head east on I-8 before exiting at Taylor Street and turning left onto Presidio Drive. This leads through Presidio Park, where the

2019 Encinitas

Cardiff-by-the-Sea

2020

2022 Solana Beach

Del Mar

2024

2035 La Jolla

San Diego

2049

US - Mexican Border

Tijuana

2066

Spanish colonists of the "Sacred Expedition" (see pages 98–99) set up their first outpost in May 1769. Two months later, a Mission was established at the same spot; it was subsequently relocated six miles to the east, but the military fortifications remained in position here, expanding as the garrison grew. By the 1820s, however, senior officers were starting to occupy the adjacent land to the south that later became San Diego's Old Town district (its Plaza contains a former commander's house, La Casa de Estudillo, built in 1827); and within a few years, the Presidio had fallen into disuse and disrepair. Near where it once stood is the Junípero Serra Museum, which displays an extensive range of artifacts excavated from its ruins.

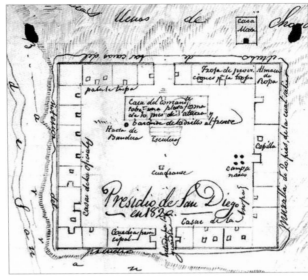

Left and below: The Junípero Serra Museum, 2727 Presidio Drive, San Diego. Despite its appearance, this is a comparatively modern structure, built in the 'Mission Revival' style and opened in 1929. The document shown on the left is a rough plan, dating from 1820, of the old Presidio.

Clockwise from right: San Diego's Sunset Cliffs; the Mission San Diego de Alcalá; the Hotel del Coronado; and Tony Curtis and Jack Lemmon 'in costume' for the movie Some Like It Hot.

After exploring San Diego's Presidio Hill, and the Old Town district just to its south (reached from Presidio Park via Jackson and Mason Streets), continue east on I-8 to its Mission Gorge Road exit. Head north on Mission Gorge, and then take a left turn onto Twain Avenue/San Diego Mission Road

towards the Mission San Diego de Alcalá. Moved here from the Presidio in 1774, the Mission—California's first—suffered a devastating Indian attack the following year, during which its Pastor, Father Luis Jayme, was martyred, and the entire settlement destroyed by fire. Though swiftly reconstructed under the auspices of its founder, Father Junípero Serra, it never attained the wealth and productivity of its more northerly counterparts, and had to be rebuilt once again after a severe earthquake in 1803. Its present church is a twentieth century restoration of the one completed in 1813; Father Jayme's remains are interred beneath its altar.

We now return, via I-8, to I-5, and resume our journey through modern San Diego. 5 first runs southeast, skirting the Old Town, Uptown and Middletown districts as it approaches Park Boulevard; this is the exit for Balboa Park, whose

1,200 acres boast a rich array of gardens, pavilions and museums, and are also home to the city's celebrated zoo. The freeway bends south here: to its right, Broadway and Market Street lead to the "Gaslamp Quarter" that was San Diego's original, post-Mexican era New Town (see pages 170–171).

The Hotel del Coronado

The Hotel del Coronado, commissioned by the Coronado Beach Company, and built by Indiana-based architects James W. Reid and his brother Watson, was completed in just eleven months, and opened in February 1888. Its lavish scale, oceanfront location, and luxurious design made it the focal point of the flourishing Coronado Island resort, and its 399 rooms and suites (subsequently expanded to 680) were soon attracting distinguished guests. These included President Benjamin Harrison (the first of 10 U.S. presidents to have stayed at the hotel), and L. Frank Baum, author of The Wizard of Oz, *who described it as the "loveliest of Eldorados." By the 1920s, the "Hotel Del" was playing host to aviator Charles Lindbergh and Edward, Prince of Wales (later King Edward VIII); and its fame received a further boost when, in 1958, director Billy Wilder filmed his Oscar-nominated movie* Some Like It Hot *there with Marilyn Monroe, Tony Curtis and Jack Lemmon. Proclaimed a National Historic Landmark in 1977, the Hotel has recently undergone a $55 million refurbishment, and continues to win awards for its accommodation and cuisine.*

Soon, we approach a junction with Highway 75, which crosses the Bay via the elegantly curved San Diego –Coronado Bridge, while 5 sweeps on to San Ysidro and the Mexican border. The route over the water (the last of our detours on this journey!) provides a fascinating glimpse of Coronado Island—a former whaling harbor developed, in the 1880s, by a shrewd group of entrepreneurs who transformed it into an upscale residential and resort community, and created the world-famous Hotel del Coronado on its Orange Avenue.

The Mexican Border

Below: Mexican novelty glassware – including a 'Stars and Stripes' loveheart.

The California/Mexico border lies some 13 miles south of San Diego. I-5 leads directly there; alternatively, take Highway 75 from Coronado, and reconnect with 5 east of Imperial Beach.

Crossing into Baja California is usually swift and straightforward (see next two pages); but the more stringent identity checks made on re-entering the USA reflect ongoing American concerns over the persistent problem of illegal migrant workers from the south. For generations, the only route to better wages and prospects for some impoverished Mexican farmhands *(braceros)* and other job seekers has lain across the border; and, following the establishment

Above: A typical tourist-oriented stall at the corner of Tijuana's Avenida Revolución and Emilio Zapata. As our other photographs show, there is no shortage of sombreros and other novelty goods around the city's central area!

of an official "guest worker" scheme for them in 1942, *braceros* became an accepted and essential part of the labor force in California and beyond.

However, since the ending of this program in 1964, employers and officials have faced a dilemma: they recognize the vital importance of Mexican workers to the US economy, but have striven, without great success, to curb spiraling levels of undocumented migration. The solution, according to

some leading politicians, is the introduction of a new registration and "regularization of status" policy. This would (in the words of former Texas Senator Phil Gramm) allow unauthorized employees "to come out of the shadows [and] work with dignity," and is currently under consideration by Presidents George W. Bush and Vicente Fox.

Above: Mexican farmworkers pictured by Harry Pennington in 1948.

Border traffic, of course, runs in both directions: Americans' desire to savor Mexican life has brought millions of dollars into Baja California Norte, and contributed to the spectacular rise of Tijuana—a former cattle ranch that began to take shape as a town in the late nineteenth century. By the late 1880s, it was possible to ride the National City & Otay Railway south from San Diego to Tijuana Junction, and within a few decades, more extensive train and highway links were bringing streams of visitors to the city's hotels, racetracks and casinos. More recently, it has developed into a busy industrial center as well as a key tourist destination, and its population reached the million mark in the 1990s.

> " There's a place, so I've been told,
> Every street is paved with gold,
> And it's just across the borderline. "
>
> *Ry Cooder, John Hiatt and Jim Dickinson,*
> **Across The Borderline,** *1980*

Below (left and right): Inevitably, much of downtown Tijuana is dominated by retail outlets, bars and eateries. Sometimes, food, drink, and tourist goods can all be found on the same premises – as at the shopping mall on the corner of Revolución and Juárez seen here.

For short excursions to Tijuana, it is easiest to catch one of the buses that leave regularly for the city from the parking lots on the American side of the border. The problems associated with driving into Mexico oneself are considerable: US car insurance is invalid there, most hired vehicles cannot be taken across the international boundary, and anyone unaccustomed to navigating the busy streets of central Tijuana would do best to avoid the experience. Border entry requirements, by contrast, are relatively straightforward, and are explained in detail overleaf. (Readers should check for any changes to existing conditions.)

On our brief ride downtown, we pass vacant lots and run-down buildings before crossing the Rio Tijuana en route for the Terminal Turística, between 6th and 7th Streets on the city's main drag, Avenida Revolución. Outside, hucksters and barkers pounce eagerly on newly arrived tourists, offering cheap trinkets, and shouting recommendations for surrounding stores and bars. Ignore them, and head left down Revolución to explore its shops and stalls for yourself; there are interesting and worthwhile goods, including locally crafted pottery, clothing and jewelry, to be found among the novelties and dubious souvenirs.

Right, and far right: A surprisingly peaceful-looking restaurant on Avenida Revolución. The road leads to Plaza Revolución, with its huge 'Arco & Reloj Monumental' (monumental arch and clock).

US brand names and restaurant chains (Coke, Pepsi, McDonald's) are strongly in evidence here, though the garish storefronts and frenetic streets are far removed from the laid-back elegance of Southern California. However, the city has calmer corners, like Arguello Street, its oldest thoroughfare, just off Plaza Revolución—a cool, restful pedestrian

Above: Despite its unusual appearance, 'El Campanario' on Avenida Revolución is yet another gift shop!

precinct, and a good location from which to view the Plaza's distinctive 'Arch and Clock' monument, erected in 2001 as a symbol of 21st century Tijuana.

Looking back up Revolución from the Plaza, we can see the hills south of the city—an enticing glimpse of the Mexico beyond this brash border town, reminding us that the decision to end our journey here is an arbitrary one, and tempting us to continue for just a few more hundred (or thousand) miles down the coast… But, for now at least, the bus ticket in our hands forces us to put aside our wanderlust, and return once again to San Ysidro.

Bibliography and Resources

Brogan, Hugh: *The Penguin History of the USA* (2nd edition) (Penguin, 2001)

Caughey, John Walton: *California* (Prentice-Hall, 1940)

Cook, James, ed. Beaglehole, J.C.: *The Journals of Captain James Cook on his Voyages of Discovery* (Cambridge University Press/Hakluyt Society, 1967)

Cooke, Alistair: *Alistair Cooke's America* (BBC, 1974)

Delehanty, Randolph: *San Francisco - The Ultimate Guide* (Chronicle Books, 1989)

DeVoto, Bernard (ed.): *The Journals of Lewis and Clark* (Houghton Mifflin, 1953)

Drake, Sir Francis: *The World Encompassed* (Nicholas Bourne, 1628)

Espy, Willard R.: *Oysterville - Roads to Grandpa's Village* (University of Washington Press, 2000)

Freeth, Nick: *Route 66* (MBI, 2001)

Guinness, Sir Alec: *Blessings in Disguise* (Hamish Hamilton, 1985)

Harris, Bill: *Pacific Coast Highway - A Photographic Journey* (Crescent Books, 1991)

Herron, Don: *The Literary World of San Francisco & Its Environs* (City Lights Books, 1985)

Johnson, Paul C. & Krell, Dorothy (eds.): *The California Missions - A Pictorial History* (Sunset Books, 1979)

Kalb, Ben & Anderson, John Gottberg (eds.): *Southern California* (Apa Publications, 1988)

Kastner, Victoria: *Hearst Castle - The Biography of a Country House* (Harry R. Abrams, Inc., 2002)

Kotkin, Joel & Grabowicz, Paul: *California Inc.* (Discus Books, 1983)

Lucas, Eric: *Hidden Pacific Northwest* (6th edition) (Ulysses Press, 2002)

McNally, Dennis: *A Long Strange Trip* (Bantam Press, 2002)

Miller, Henry: *Big Sur and the Oranges of Hieronymous Bosch* (New Directions Publishing Corporation, 1957)

Morris, Jan: *Coast to Coast - A Journey Across 1950s America* (Travelers' Tales, 2002)

Nevins, Allan & Commager, Henry Steele, with Morris, Jeffrey: *A Pocket History of the United States* (9th edition) (Pocket Books, 1992)

Nordhoff, Charles: *California: For Health, Pleasure and Residence* (Harper & Row, 1873)

O'Brien, Robert: *This is San Francisco* (Chronicle Books, 1994)

Rhein, Michael J.: *Anatomy of the Lighthouse* (Saraband, 2001)

Riegert, Ray: *Hidden San Francisco and North California* (6th edition) (Ulysses Press, 1994)

Rindge, Frederick Hastings: *Happy Days in Southern California* (n.p., 1898)

Steinbeck, John: *Cannery Row* (Viking Press, 1945)

Stevenson, Robert Louis: *Across the Plains* (Nelson, 1879)

Thompson, Peter: *Cassell's Dictionary of American History* (Cassell, 2002)

Ward, Greg (ed.): *USA - The Rough Guide* (The Rough Guides, 1994)

Weir, Kim: *Coastal California* (Moon Handbooks, 2000)

USEFUL ADDRESSES AND INTERNET LINKS

CHAPTER ONE
Olympic National Park headquarters:
600 East Park Avenue
Port Angeles, WA 98362
www.nps.gov/olym

North Olympic Peninsula Visitor & Convention Bureau
P.O. Box 670
338 W. First Street #104
Port Angeles, WA 98362
www.olympicpeninsula.org

Makah Nation website
www.makah.com

The Polson Museum
1611 Riverside Avenue
P.O. Box 432
Hoquiam, WA 98550
www.polsonmuseum.org

Grays Harbor Chamber of Commerce
506 Duffy Street
Aberdeen, WA 98520
www.graysharbor.org

Brady's Oysters
3714 Oyster Place E.
Aberdeen, WA 98520
users.techline.com/broyster/

Cranberry Coast Chamber of Commerce
www.cranberrycoastcoc.com

Tokeland Hotel
100 Hotel Road
Tokeland, WA 98690
www.tokelandhotel.com

Raymond Chamber of Commerce
P.O. Box 86
Raymond, WA 98577
www.visit.willapabay.org

Pacific County Courthouse
300 Memorial Drive
P.O. Box 86
South Bend, WA 98586

Long Beach Peninsula Visitors Bureau
P.O. Box 562
Long Beach, WA 98631
www.funbeach.com

Fort Canby State Park (and Lewis and Clark Interpretive Center)
PO Box 488
Ilwaco, WA 98624
lewisandclarktrail.com/section4/wacities/chinook/lewisclarkcenter/

CHAPTER TWO
Astoria-Warrenton Area Chamber of Commerrce
111 West Marine Drive
P.O. Box 176
Astoria, OR 97103
www.oldoregon.com

Fort Clatsop National Mem.
www.nps.gov/focl/

Seaside Visitor's Bureau
7 N. Roosevelt
Seaside, OR 97138
www.seasideor.com

Tillamook Cheese Visitor Center
4175 Highway 101 N.
P.O. Box 313
Tillamook, OR 97141

Lincoln City Visitor and Convention Bureau
801 SW Highway 101 Suite 1
Lincoln City, OR 97367
www.oregoncoast.org

Flying Dutchman Winery
P.O. Box 308
Otter Rock, OR 97369
www.dutchmanwinery.com

Greater Newport Chamber of Commerce
555 S.W. Coast Highway
Newport, OR 97365

Rogue Ales
2320 OSU Drive
Newport, OR 97365
www.rogue.com

Sea Lion Caves
91560 Hwy. 101 N.
Florence, OR 97439
www.sealioncaves.com

Florence Chamber of Commerce
270 Hwy 101
Florence, Oregon 97439
www.florencechamber.com

Coos Bay Area Chamber of Commerce
50 Central Avenue
Coos Bay, OR 97420

188

Bandon Chamber of Commerce
300 S. 2nd Street
P.O. Box 1515C
Bandon-by-the-Sea, OR 97411
www.bandon.com

Gold Beach Visitor Center
29279 Ellensburg #3
P.O. Box 375
Gold Beach, OR 97444
www.goldbeach.org

Rogue River Mail Boat Trips
P.O. Box 1165-G
Gold Beach, OR 97444
www.mailboat.com

For information on State
Parks and lighthouses:
Oregon State Parks
1115 Commercial Street NE,
Suite 1
Salem, OR 97301-1002
www.oregonstateparks.org

CHAPTER THREE
Redwood National Park
1111 Second Street
Crescent City, CA 95531
www.redwood.national-park.com

Trees of Mystery
P.O. Box 96
Klamath, CA 95548
www.treesofmystery.com

Humboldt County
Convention & Vistors
Bureau
www.redwoodvisitor.org

Humboldt Brewery
856 10th Street
Arcata, CA 95521
www.humbrew.com

Ferndale Chamber of
Commerce
P.O. Box 325
Ferndale, CA 95536
www.victorianferndale.org/chamber

Californian Western Skunk
Train (from Fort Bragg to
Willits)
P.O.Box 907
Fort Bragg, CA 95437
www.skunktrain.com

North Coast Brewing Co.
455 N. Main Street
Fort Bragg, CA 95437

Mendocino Coast Chamber
of Commerce
332 North Main Street
PO Box 1141
Fort Bragg, CA 95437
www.mendocinocoast2.com

Fort Ross State Historic Park
19005 Coast Highway 1
Jenner, CA 95503
www.mcn.org/1/rrparks/fort ross

Point Reyes National
Seashore Association
Point Reyes Station CA
94956
www.ptreyes.org

Muir Woods National
Monument
Mill Valley, CA 94941-2696
www.nps.gov/muwo

For information on State
Parks:
California State Parks
P.O. Box 942896
Sacramento, CA 94296-0001
www.parks.ca.gov

CHAPTER FOUR
San Francisco Visitor
Information Center
900 Market Street
San Francisco, CA 94103-2804
www.sfvisitor.org

Santa Cruz Beach Boardwalk
400 Beach Street
Santa Cruz, CA 95060
www.beachboardwalk.com

Laguna Seca Recreation Area
1025 Monterey, Hwy. 68
Salinas, CA 93908
(Raceway homepage):
www.laguna-seca.com

Monterey County
Convention & Visitors Bureau
P.O.Box 1770
Monterey, CA 93942
www.montereyinfo.org

CHAPTER FIVE
Carmel California Visitor &
Information Center
San Carlos, between 5th & 6th
Carmel-by-the-Sea, CA 93921
www.carmelcalifornia.org

The Tuck Box
Post Office Box TT
Carmel-by-the-Sea, CA 93921
www.tuckbox.com

Ragged Point Inn and Resort
19019 Highway 1
Ragged Point, CA 93452
www.raggedpointinn.com

Hearst San Simeon State
Historical Monument
(Hearst Castle)
750 Hearst Castle Road
San Simeon, CA 93452
www.hearst-castle.org

San Simeon State Park
San Simeon Creek Road
Cambria, CA 93452
www.parks.ca.gov

San Luis Obispo County
Visitors & Conference
Bureau
1037 Mill Street
San Luis Obispo, CA 93401
www.SanLuisObispoCounty.com

SLO Brewing Co.
1119 Garden Street
San Luis Obispo, CA 93401
www.slobrew.com

Madonna Inn
100 Madonna Road
San Luis Obispo, CA 93405
www.madonnainn.com

City of Lompoc
100 Civic Center Plaza
Lompoc, CA 93438
www.ci.lompoc.ca.us

Santa Barbara Conference &
Visitors Bureau and Film
Commission
1601 Anacapa Street
Santa Barbara, CA 93101-1909
www.santabarbaraca.com

CHAPTER SIX
City of Santa Monica official
homepage
www.santa-monica.org/cm/

Venice Area Chamber of
Commerce
P.O. Box 202
Venice, CA 90294
venice.net/chamber/

Wayfarers Chapel
5755 Palos Verdes Drive
South
Rancho Palos Verdes, CA
90275
www.wayfarerschapel.org

RMS 'Queen Mary' official
website
www.queenmary.com

City of Long Beach tourist
website
www.visitlongbeach.com

Huntington Beach official
website
www.ci.huntington-beach.ca.us

CHAPTER SEVEN
City of San Clemente
100 Avenida Presidio
San Clemente, CA 92672
Internet (tourist

information): *ci.san-clemente.ca.us/org/CityNews/Calendar/default.asp*

City of Carlsbad official
website – visitors' pages
www.ci.carlsbad.ca.us/visit/index.html

Quail Botanical Gardens
230 Quail Gardens Drive
Encinitas, CA 92023
www.qbgardens.com

Del Mar Fairgrounds
2260 Jimmy Durante
Boulevard
Del Mar, CA 92014
www.delmarfair.com

San Diego Convention &
Visitors Bureau
11 Horton Plaza
San Diego, CA 92101
www.sandiego.org

Hotel Del Mar
1500 Orange Avenue
Coronado, CA 92118
www.hoteldel.com

Traveling into Mexico
US citizens entering Mexico
from San Ysidro must carry
proof of citizenship (e.g.
passport, voter registration
card, birth certificate). Other
visitors (including
Canadians) must carry
passports.

These regulations apply to
tourists making visits of less
than 72 hours to Mexico's
border cities from the USA;
there are different
requirements and conditions
for longer stays and more
extensive travel. If in doubt,
check with the Mexican
authorities, and/or your own
country's consulate.

Index

Acknowledgements

The author would like to thank all the individuals and organizations who were so generous with their assistance and advice during the preparation and writing of this book. Special thanks to Bill DuBois (our pilot in Washington State), and to Vern and ReRun at Willapa Harbor Airport; Hoyt Fields and Dan Eller at Hearst Castle; Bill Harris; Janet Holmes; Paul Johnson and Rick Cordell; Mary Lou Lorensen; and Alan Sussex.

Finally, a special vote of thanks to Neil Sutherland for his photography, his patience, and his willingness to drive over 3,000 miles across America with me to gather material.

"The Lone Cypress" and "17-Mile Drive" are registered trademarks of the Pebble Beach Company.

"Hearst Castle," "La Cuesta Encantada," "The Enchanted Hill," and "Hearst San Simeon State Historical Monument" are registered trademarks of Hearst Castle®/CA State Parks.

Quotation on p.16 from Hugh Brogan, *The Penguin History of the USA*. Publisher: Penguin; © 1985, 1999 Addison Wesley Longman

Quotation on p.25 from Jan Morris, *Coast to Coast*. Publisher: Travelers' Tales (San Francisco); © 1956 Jan Morris

Quotation on p.33 from Willard R. Espy, *Oysterville – Roads to Grandpa's Village*. Publisher: University of Washington Press; © 1977 Willard R. Espy

Quotation on p.101 from Malvina Reynolds, *Little Boxes* © 1962 Schroder Music Co. (ASCAP), Renewed 1990. Used by permission. All rights reserved.

Quotation on p.111 from Ray Riegert, *Hidden San Francisco and Northern California*. Publisher: Ulysses Press; © 1984 Ray Riegert

Quotation on p.113 from John Steinbeck, *Cannery Row*. Publisher: Penguin; © 1945 John Steinbeck

Quotation on p.129 from Henry Miller, *Big Sur and the Oranges of Hieronymus Bosch*. Publisher: New Directions Publishing Corporation; © 1957 New Directions Publishing Corporation

Quotation on p.135 from Alec Guinness, *Blessings in Disguise*.

Publisher Hamish Hamilton, © 1985 Alec Guinness

Quotation on p.154 from Alistair Cooke, *Alistair Cooke's America*. Publisher: BBC; © 1973 Alistair Cooke

Quotation on p.185 from Ry Cooder, John Hiatt and Jim Dickinson, *Across The Borderline*. © 1980 Duchess Music Corporation/ MCA Music Publishing

Archive photos of Washington on pages 12 (top left), 17 (right), 26 (right), 29 (right), 31 (right) and 76 (right) courtesy of the Pacific County Historical Society, www.pacificcohistory.org

Photo of Oysterville Church (p.32 bottom left) by Wayne O'Neil, courtesy of Long Beach Peninsula Visitors Bureau

Photo of James Dean (p.134 top left) courtesy of The Kobal Collection

Photo of Capitol Records Building (p.155 top right) and Pier at San Clemente State Beach (p.174-5 middle) courtesy of © Richard Cummins/CORBIS

Photo of Neimans Restaurant in Carlsbad (p.170 right) © Ralf Brown www.pbase.com/ralf

Photos of Richard & Pat Nixon (p. 174 left) courtesy U.S. National Archives

Nixon postcard and photo of Casa Romantica (p. 175) courtesy of the Heritage of San Clemente Foundation

Photo of Alt Karlsbad and Carlsbad Train Station (p.176) courtesy of © Ralf Brown www.pbase.com/ralf

Photos of Quail Gardens (p.178) courtesy of © Lowell J. Greenberg www.earthrenewal.org

Harry Pennington's photo of Mexican farmworkers (p.185) courtesy of Hulton Archive

The publishers gratefully acknowledge permission to reproduce copyright material. Every effort has been made to contact original sources and copyright holders for permissions. In case of any omissions, please contact Salamander Books Ltd.